SEBRING

The First Decade

by *Barry Foster*

The First in a Series

No part of this publication may be reproduced in whole or in part, or stored in a retrieval system, or transmitted in any form or by any means, electronic, mechanical, photocopying, recording, or otherwise, without written permission of the author, except for the inclusion of brief quotations in a review. For information regarding permission, please write to: info@barringerpublishing.com.

Copyright © 2025 BARRY FOSTER
All rights reserved.

Barringer Publishing, Naples, Florida
www.barringerpublishing.com
Design and layout by Linda S. Duider

Cover photo reprinted with permission of the Sebring Historical Society

ISBN 978-1-954396-82-1

Library of Congress Cataloging-in-Publication Data
Sebring: The First Decade
The First in a Series

Printed in U.S.A.

This book is dedicated to those who helped to create the 12 Hours of Sebring, those who helped perpetuate and grow this wonderful event, and especially to the fans who turn out each March to celebrate.

Reprinted with permission of the Sebring Historical Society.

CONTENTS

FOREWORD..................................iv

INTRODUCTION 1

Chapter 1
    1950—The Sam Collier Memorial.......... 13

Chapter 2
    1952—The First 12 Hours................. 23

Chapter 3
    1953—The Grand Prix of Endurance 33

Chapter 4
    1954—A Historic Upset................... 41

Chapter 5
    1955—A Truly International Race......... 53

Chapter 6
    1956—The ARCF Emerges................. 65

Chapter 7
    1957 79

Chapter 8
1958 93

Chapter 9
1959 107

Chapter 10
1960 125

Chapter 11
1961—A Decade in the Books 133

EPILOGUE/CONCLUSION. 145

ACKNOWLEDGEMENTS 152

FOREWORD

I've had the privilege of listening to Barry Foster for years as a local radio host, but it has been over the past decade, while collaborating on projects about the history of the 12 Hours of Sebring, that I've truly come to appreciate the depth of his knowledge and passion for the race. Barry is more than just a dedicated historian; he is an integral part of the Sebring racing community. Few people on this Earth have spent as much time discussing, promoting, and preserving the legacy of the 12 Hours of Sebring as he has over the past 40 years.

The history of this beloved race has been a focal point of my life, and I've spent countless hours researching its many facets. While there are numerous books and articles devoted to the 12 Hours of Sebring, the one thing I've always felt was missing is the perspective of the local Sebring citizens. These are the people who made the race possible year in and year out. Without them, we would not have the iconic event we know today.

Barry Foster has done something truly special with this work—he has gone beyond the cars, the drivers, and the spectators to uncover the "behind the scenes" action that makes race week run so smoothly. His research delves into the contributions of local clubs who sold concessions at the circuit, to the Sebring Firemen, Inc. who helped sanction the race, and to the countless others whose work and dedication to the event often go unnoticed.

This book is not just about the history of the 12 Hours of Sebring; it's a tribute to the people of Sebring. Barry's in-depth exploration reminds us that the race is not just an international motorsport event; it's a testament to the spirit of community and the unsung heroes who have worked tirelessly to make it what it is today.

I am honored to introduce this important work to you. Whether you are a lifelong Sebring fan or someone discovering the race for the first time, I have no doubt that you will be moved by the rich, local history that Barry has so expertly captured here.

Enjoy the journey through the eyes of Sebring's most resolute supporters.

INTRODUCTION

The 12 Hours of Sebring. The name conjures up the image of a long day's journey into night, as flites of sports cars of every description challenge a racetrack carved from the runways and access roads of an historic airport in central Florida.

From a small gathering of amateur sports car enthusiasts, 'The Race' has grown into one of the most prestigious such events in the world.

Sebring pioneer, Alan Altvader, who ended up being a pivotal figure in the creation of the Sebring sports car race, noted that the central Florida community was no stranger to racing events. As early as 1916, power boat regattas had been staged on Lake Jackson, and there had been sailboat races on the lake as well. Other competitions included a brief spate of horse races, marathon foot races, and even "Gopher Derbies" managed by another Sebring pioneer—Sophie Mae Mitchell. Altvader noted that these had gained "national attention."

In fact, there had even been automobile races on the unpaved streets of the city. He noted that with such a variety of such activity, ". . . there was little objection to the sports car lobby." The creation of the 12 Hours of Sebring as a grand prix endurance race for sports cars came together as a series of events and a melding of individuals and groups in quite an unlikely manner. The idea of this style of racing was in many ways a natural extension of the post World War II era. Many of the young men returning from the service were more than familiar with European auto makes. Foreign sports cars really weren't so foreign to most of America, who had followed the troops in Britain, France, Italy, and Germany. In fact, the world was coming together, and the United States was in a growth period—more money, and more leisure time. And of course, the Sebring airport had started life as Hendricks Field, a training base for B-17 bomber pilots and crews.

The Sports Car Club of America was born, and races were held in the more traditional, European style. Not sanctioned by any racing organization, but more as friendly sport—to test one's car and racing skills against one's peers. The early races were as much for pride and comradery as anything else.

The selection of the Sebring air terminal as a race site may actually have stemmed from a 1950s race that was planned to stage at Palm Beach Shores. That competition was to have run in the streets of West Palm Beach—much the same as the Monte Carlo rally.

However, a local promotor who conducted speedway and stock car races on a half-mile track near there, reportedly created agitation amongst the city fathers prior to event, telling them there would be "blood in the streets" if the cars were allowed to race. Later, organizers moved the race to an undeveloped housing project planned for

Palm Beach Shores. The "Race Around the Houses," as it was billed, was won by George Huntoon in a Ford/Duesenberg.

While it was deemed a success, members of the newly formed Sports Car Club of America continued to look for both a more private and a more permanent site, where they could continue their competition in peace.

Many sports car races were organized and held in remote locations, because at the time, crowds were seen to be of nuisance value. These races were supposed to be competitions among amateurs, who did it not for money but for the love of the sport. Just as the famous Watkins Glen is off the beaten track, so was the central Florida hamlet of Sebring.

Among other hats he wore, longtime resident and Sebring fireman, Allen Altvader, was the manager at the Sebring Air Terminal in the late '40s and early '50s. As he tells the story—it was one day in 1949, that a plane landed at his facility and two men asked to see the person in charge. One was Sam Collier, the other apparently was Bob Gegen. They said that they had flown over, viewed the site from the air, and asked if it would be possible to hold a race on the grounds there.

"They gave me the impression that they were a couple of millionaire playboys that had been associated with a lot of other men of their stripe," said Altvader, "They had raced at Watkins Glen, New York, and what they wanted to do was to compete against each other."

Apparently, the two did not have plans to hold a race for the public, but they had asked about setting up a circuit for practice road races. The three men took a ride around the facility by car, asking questions and talking about the possibilities.

Altvader recalled that it did not appear that the two had reached any kind of planning phase, but it was more in the nature of something they would like to get organized. "A trip around the airport by car appeared to convince them that the facilities were adequate," he said.

When asked if the field would be available, Altvader informed them that the decision would be up to Sebring's city council, who had the final say over activities at the air terminal. "Well, the two got in their plane and left," he said, "and that's the last I ever saw of Sam Collier.

Collier went to Watkins Glen and was killed in 1950 while leading the competition behind the wheel of a Ferrari. However, before the race started, Collier had announced to the drivers that there were plans to hold a race at the Sebring airfield.

Nevertheless, Altvater noted that local officials continued negotiations with Phil Stiles and George Huntoon to stage a race at the airfield. Altvader said he later spoke with city council members individually to see if they'd have any objection to a sports car race being staged at the air terminal, however, there actually was nothing done toward physically developing it.

One of the founding members of the SCCA was a man named Alec Ulmann. He had been a member of the Automobile Racing Club of America, and a long-time road racing enthusiast. He had spoken to Collier and Gegen about their trip over Sebring's de-commissioned bomber training field, and saw the opportunity to create a circuit, in much the same way that the English had converted their aerodromes for sports car road racing.

Ulman was a prominent figure in both the sports car and aviation industries in the US and abroad. He took the opportunity to tour the Sebring facility while looking for hangar space and apron facilities for the building and storage of aircraft. He had been converting military planes to civilian use, and overhauling others for the military of smaller nations. Ulman had flown to Sebring to confer with Col. Claude D. Richardson.

Col. Richardson had a facility at the Sebring Air Terminal that sold surplus war assets administration materials. They had 17 warehouses on the field, receiving shipments by boxcar, then selling them off. He had many contacts with wealthy and influential people, and it was in September 1950 that Phil Stiles came back with a man by the name of George Huntoon. The men took up where Gegen and Collier had left off the year before, except that they introduced the idea of the Sports Car Club of America being involved.

"In 1949, the club was not mentioned at all," said Altvader, "this was just to be a friendly get-together of a bunch of fellas."

This presented a different situation, although they still didn't particularly care for spectators, the race organizers needed sponsors to give prizes. They also needed permission from the city to use the grounds and, more importantly, they needed a means to keep people—or animals—from wandering out onto the course. The only group in town that could measure up to that task were the Sebring Firemen, Inc. They had a membership of about a hundred young men who would be of the right age and disposition to manage that part of such an endeavor.

So, it was agreed that if they held a race, the firemen would set up the field, and the racers would organize the actual competition. To make it worth their while, the sports car club agreed if the firemen wanted to put a gate on and collect admission charges that they could have any money that evolved out of that.

The Sebring Chamber of Commerce also pledged their cooperation. As the manager of the air terminal, Altvader sent this memorandum to the council members:

> To the members of the City Council:
>
> No doubt you will be asked in the near future for approval of an agreement to operate a road race on the Air Terminal on 31 December of this year, to be sponsored by Sebring Firemen, Inc. This is the same activity to which you gave your consent approximately two years ago and is under the same management as that which has been operated for the past three years at Watkins Glen, New York, in the Summertime.
>
> It is our understanding that through the cooperation of Mr. C. D. Richardson of the American Industrial Sales Corporation, the sponsors will have adequate financing

and manpower to do all the work needed to actually run the race and I presume that some arrangements will be made to provide physical improvements that are needed to prepare for such an event. As you know, the finances of the Terminal will not permit any extensive expenditures at this particular time although we are prepared to do a certain amount of work which would be normally done at some time or other such as clearing the runways of weeds and the minor amount of repairs to streets. However, should work be necessary beyond which we would normally expect to do, we would not have the money for that purpose in our funds and arrangements would have to be made using some other manner. For the work we would expect to do we would also have to ask for the use of road repair equipment.

    We would like to cooperate heartily with the Sebring Firemen in this venture as we have always believed that it would be of incalculable value to the town as a whole, not only from the view of furnishing much-needed tourist entertainment but it would bring a great deal of money into the town to hotels, restaurants, filling stations and garages at a time when they are not overcrowded.

It is also our understanding that such a race would give widespread national publicity to the community from several different angles, and it was planned for a date when many would be enroute to Miami for the New Year's game and would probably stop overnight here for this event. We see only a few disadvantages.

No doubt the general chairman of the event, Mr. Forrest Howard will approach the Council at an early date seeking permission to enter into a contract with the management and we would strongly recommend that such a contract be authorized subject to a provision to hold the city harmless in the event of loss or accident.

A. Altvader

The idea was greeted with less than wild enthusiasm. The council members were worried about the liabilities—financial or physical—associated with such an event and ended up giving the firemen permission to use the field.

Ulmann, described by *Speed Sport News* editor, Chris Economacki, as "an internationalist," moved ahead; he saw in Sebring the fulfillment of a dream.

Born in Russia, Ulmann was a Continental. For quite some time he had been enthralled with the *Le Mans* circuit in France—considered the consummate test of speed and endurance in a 24-hour race.

In his book, *The Sebring Story*, he says he had been looking for a way to replicate the kinds of roads encountered at his *Le Mans*. And, apparently, he'd found it at the Sebring air terminal.

Ulmann outlined his vision as:

"Two glorious one-mile straightaways, so necessary for top speed competition, [and other roads that] could simulate *Le Mans'* right angle turns of *Mulsane* and *Arnage*, and the 200 mph straight passes at the *Hinaudieres*."

He said it had been a constant source of disappointment for him to see American racing forced by promoters into what he termed "the dead end of round or oval racing" way from the tradition of the Vanderbilt Cup races on Long Island, New York . . . or like competitions on regular road courses.

With the help of Sam Collier and SCCA Region Director Bob Gegen, a 3.5-mile course was laid out, utilizing two of the airfield's runways.

Ulman's goal was a sort of "little *Le Mans*"—a six-hour race that would be run on the index of performance. The index of performance was a complicated formula which was designed as an equalizer between large and small displacement cars as a means to determine the overall performance of a vehicle by taking a number of factors into account. Ulman boasted that he had contrived the "purist idea" of naming the winner based on this formula, "thereby completely befuddling the few local spectators who were enticed to come to the event." It all added to the profound mystery of what this was all about.

The race would be the first European style road race to be held in the United States and would be run under international rules. However, Ulmann failed to achieve the needed FIA sanctioning and reportedly was told by the President of Commission Sportive, Monsieur Augustin Perouse, that the FIA had been firmly committed to the Contest Board of the American Automobile Association and Col. Arthur Herringtion. Herrington staged another famous race, the Indianapolis 500.

But the group pressed on. Spurred by the death of Sam Collier, they decided to run it as much as a tribute to their friend and compatriot as it was to be the start of this kind of competition in America.

Said Ulmann, "No better name, no greater honor could have been bestowed on that inaugural attempt to re-create Lemans." [sic] And with that, the first faint beginnings of the tradition that would eventually evolve into the 12 Hours of Sebring were born.

Race creator and promoter **Alec Ulmann** at the microphone at the Sam Collier Memorial. The inaugural six-hour race was the precursor of the series which has become the Mobil 1 12 Hours of Sebring. (Bill Foster Collection)

This is the **Crosley Hot Shot** that won the inaugural race at Sebring, the Sam Collier Memorial. It bested much faster cars by winning on the "index of performance." The formula was designed to take the car's weight and engine displacement to figure the maximum number of laps it should be able to complete within the time of the race. (Bill Foster Collection)

1950—The Sam Collier Memorial

It was announced in the *Highlands County News* of November 10, 1950, that an automobile race had been booked at the Sebring Air Terminal. The Sam Collier Memorial Trophy Grand Prix of Endurance would be run on December 31st.

The event was to be a six-hour race for sports cars meeting the mechanical requirements of the International Automobile l' Association whose headquarters were in Paris, France. Said the paper, ". . . this thrilling event is the longest race to be held in the United States in many years."

The idea was to snag fans on their way to the Orange Bowl football game in Miami. It didn't work.

"We learned that the people who liked football were not necessarily the ones who liked car racing," said Sebring

Historian and former air terminal manager Alan Altvader, "so later the date was changed."

The race was co-sponsored by the Sebring Firemen, Inc., and the Sports Car Club of America. The city was represented by a three-man committee comprised of Col. C.D. Richardson, Gatchell Burton, and H.T. Hagemeister. The SCCA listed a similar three-member committee with President D. Cameron Peck, contest board chairman William F. Milliken Jr. and activities committee chairman, Alec Ulman, acting as their representatives.

Phil Stiles was tapped as the General Race Chairman. Stiles said he helped Bob Gegen and Sam Collier lay out the original 3.5-mile circuit at the air terminal. "We tried to make it an interesting course," said Stiles in an interview later, "but everything had to be on the outside because there were no bridges or other means to get to the infield area."

Dick Sullivan of Boston managed public relations for the first event. He told local reporters that the Sebring race had been planned as a smaller version of the famous *Le Mans* 24-hour grand prix. Another Boston area concern, R.G. Began Company, reportedly was given rights to the concessions. Began said he had already arranged for two major film companies to take newsreel footage of the inaugural event.

Promoter Alec Ulmann's wife, Mary, who had served as the Race Secretary at Watkins Glen, prepared the regulations. Ulmann said the first competition was run "more reminiscent of a family contest." Apparently, there was no attempt made to notify existing national or international racing bodies other than Ulmann's unfruitful attempt with the FIA. Nonetheless, on race day there was a much larger contingent of enthusiasts on hand than expected by organizers.

This was to be the first time a day and night road race would be presented in America. Newspaper accounts termed the layout ". . . one of the trickiest in the country."

Reporters wrote that "the city of Sebring has taken on all the feverish excitement, color, and appearance of Race Week in Indianapolis as owners, drivers, mechanics, and spectators are streaming in for the first Sam Collier Memorial Grand Prix."

The first man to travel over the course was listed as owner/driver William Spear of Manchester, New Hampshire. He hit a top reported speed of 128 miles per hour in a Ferrari. The second contestant to try the new track was Erwin Goldschmidt of New York City. He turned a top end of 144 mph in a Cadillac Allard two-seater.

Fans were permitted on the grounds for half price on Friday to witness the time trials. Dignitaries in attendance included then Florida Governor Fuller Warren, who was to function as the honorary starter. He rode around the track before the race with SCCA Regional Executive Director George Huntoon at speeds reaching an estimated 110 mph. Afterward he quipped to reporters, "This is not nearly as hazardous as some political races!"

Radio personality Arthur Godfrey was invited to attend, and the aerobatic women's champion, Betty Skelton, of Tampa was to perform aerial maneuvers in her midget plane.

Although sports car enthusiasts had designed the course, it was the Sebring Firemen that did the actual set up work at the track. "We had no real experience in this area," said Alan Altvader, "but that shortcoming was offset by a deep dedication to 'get the show on the road.'" The firemen had no treasury balance to set up a racing operation, but they did have excellent credit and used it to the limit. The group had hoped to raise the money back through ticket and program sales.

When it was time to race, the scene was a primitive one. There were no real pits, just wooden tables joined together with two-by-four boards. They had been provided by

Florida Governor Fuller Warren was taken around the track during the Sam Collier Memorial by then Executive Director of the Sports Car Club of Miami George Huntoon. The car reportedly hit a top speed of 110 mph during the excursion. After exiting the car, Governor Warren famously quipped that it was "not nearly as hazardous as some of the political races" he had endured. (Bill Foster Collection)

American Industrial Sales Corporation (C. D. Richardson's company). A report from the Sebring Historical Society's archives indicates that most of them disappeared following the race, along with the airport's fire extinguishers and even articles of lesser value.

The firemen were charged with furnishing a first aid tent, ambulances, and tow trucks. They also were to provide hay bales and oil drums to help mark out the course. It was resident Woodrow Harshman who was given the responsibility of rounding up several hundred of the barrels and he delivered. Altvader remarked that it was "a matter of wonderment to us all." He never divulged where he got them or to where they were returned.

Ham radios were used for communication on the course, there also were miles and miles of wire that were strung by resident Bill Dutton. He and his subcommittee then had to retrieve the tangled mess after the excitement was over. Gasoline was provided to the drivers without cost. It had been suggested that an oil company be contacted to furnish the fuel. In return, they would be given a full-page ad in the fireman's program, the company truck would be prominently parked, and the company's name would be displayed on a banner which would then be strung across the track. In the end, Col. Richardson used his business clout to encourage Green's "Pure Oil" distributorship of Avon Park to furnish the fuel.

Spectators were charged a nominal fee for entrance to the track. The prices were $1 for adults, and 25-cents for children. There was also a parking fee of $1 per car. Fans could either watch the race from the privacy of their auto, or sit in a grandstand, specifically erected for the event. Proceeds from the admissions were to go to the Sebring Firemen's charity fund.

Thirty-eight cars were registered for the very first Sebring race, 28 started and only 17 finished. For the first time ever in an American race, drivers used the *"Le Mans start"* that was to become the trademark of the race during the early years. Competitors were lined up opposite their vehicles, and on the signal would run across the track, jump in the driver's seat, start the engine, and take off.

Nils Michelson, the race starter, dropped the green flag at 3:00 on a sunny but cold New Year's Eve afternoon. The start of a new tradition took off with a roar.

The #16 Cadillac-Healy of Phil Walters (a.k.a. Ted Tappet on the midget racing circuit) and Bill Frick was the first car away. For the first two hours, it was the Cadillac Allards of Walters, Fred Wacker and Erwinn Goldschmidt, that were locked in a three-way duel for the lead. But the winner was a Crosley Hot Shot—the only American car entered in the race. It was driven by Ralph (Bob) DeShon and Fred (Frits) Koster.

As the story goes, Tampa resident Vic Sharpe had driven the tiny sports car to the track with no intention of racing it. In fact, Sharpe had brought some spare parts to Tommy Cole who was scheduled to drive with Goldschmidt. Alec Ulmann relates that Cole preferred to be listed out of New York rather than London, to prevent being disqualified in racing back in England. Reportedly, it was Cole who first suggested that Sharpe's car actually could win under the complicated index of performance.

Because Sharpe was not an SCCA member, Deshon and Koster were enlisted to drive the car. They helped to boost their chances with a few slight modifications. They removed the Hot Shot's bumpers and windshield to help reduce the weight, then added a piece of plexiglass as a windscreen. Apparently, the plastic was a part of one of the B-17's that had been stationed at the World War II bomber training facility there at the Hendricks Field.

They completed only 89 laps in the six-hour affair, but it proved to be an easy win under the formula. In truth, they'd led in that regard from the first hour of the race. In the sixth hour, the Hot Shot began to take some heat from "Gentleman Jim" Kimberly in a Ferrari. But teammates instructed Koster (just newly arrived from Holland) to "go faster." Their pit board was the side of an old suitcase, held up as he motored by on the straightaway. Using the gearshift, Koster was able to add an additional four mph to his lap time and cruised to victory. Kimberly, SCCA president at the time, finished second.

Two other cars, a Cadillac Allard and a Cadillac Healy, completed 20 more laps than the winners in the same six-hour time span. Ironically, the Goldschmidt/Cole effort was disqualified for accepting assistance on the track. The team was charged with allowing a mechanic to bring a key from the pit to unlock the hood. (It also was alleged that the mechanic helped check out the problem after the hood was opened.) The car was just a quarter mile from the start/finish line. Nonetheless, the town of Sebring presented Goldschmidt with a cup for "Most Competent Driver" in the race.

Two-time *Le Mans* Winner—Luigi Chenetti—traveled the greatest distance without a co-driver. He finished seventh overall in a Ferrari 166 Berlinetta. Phil Stiles said one of his duties as Race Chairman turned out to be picking up the pieces. He'd had the word "OFFICIAL" written on his car and toured the course picking up bits that had fallen off some of the vehicles.

"People weren't prepared for anything that long and most didn't even take the mufflers off," he said, "you'd be surprised what we found."

The original hay bales were not hay at all but were peanut bales that were brought down from Georgia. It rained the night before the race, and they turned hard as rock.

"It was worse than hitting those sand-filled drums they put out," said Stiles.

Officials estimated that 8,000 fans turned out for the event. However, in a subsequent report to the Sebring Firemen, treasurer Floyd Shoemaker later reported that the group had sold 2800 tickets and had given out a like number. A later analysis by Sebring historian, Allen Altvader, showed that there were practically no sales of reserved or box seats. The firemen, who had hoped to make money between the program and ticket sales, actually lost about $2,000 on the event. But Col. Richardson saved the day by purchasing a full-page ad in the program to make up the difference.

"I guess you could say as a race it was successful," said Altvader, "but as a business venture it was a flop."

Following the race, there was a New Year's party at Harder Hall. Then manager, Sally Giffard, tells of a hastily thrown together affair, with the hotel's gardener ending up as the musical entertainment. Giffard said that at the late hour, she could not find a band. And she figured the racers would be more interested in talking than in dancing. Giffard proceeded to get the man's guitar out of hock and told him ". . . you're hired." In Sunday night festivities, Governor Warren presented the first Sam Collier Memorial Trophy, and the Sebring races had their start.

Mrs. Janice Shoemaker sits atop #19 winning Crosley on Dec. 31, 1950. An awards program was held at Harder Hall after the 6-hour race. Photo by Ted Shoemaker. (Bill Foster Collection)

This is a photo from the first **12 Hours of Sebring**, as drivers gathered for their final briefing before the race. Much of the infrastructure in the background is gone. The "temporary" airport buildings built for the Hendricks Field bomber training facility have been dismantled and replaced by a modern airside center. The tower (for which Sebring's Tower Turn is named) also has been dismantled and is but a memory. The control tower remains, however. Preserved as a monument to the airport's history by the Sebring Airport Authority. (Bill Foster Collection)

1952—The First 12 Hours

Highlands county residents learned in November 1951 that the Sebring Firemen, Inc. would sponsor their second sports car endurance race at the Sebring Air Terminal. A March 7th article in the *Avon Park Sun* noted that ". . . Sebring and Highlands County may well feel proud at being selected for the International Grand Prix race . . ."

Groundwork for the event had been established during an October 26 meeting with race steward, Alec Ulmann, and Sebring Fire Chief Forrest Howard. The scheduled date would be March 15, 1952, with practice on March 13, and qualifying trials on the 14th. The first full 12-hour race at Sebring would be in 1952. Not only was it a longer race than the 1950 Sam Collier Memorial timewise, but the layout of the course was changed as well. The course was configured into the 5.2-mile pattern that more accurately reflects the course as it is known today. The famous "hairpin turn" was added as was the "Webster corner." It would remain virtually unchanged for 30 years.

Part of the new course was furnished by the Sebring Firemen, Inc. The *Highlands County News* of March 7, 1952, indicates that through them, two new roads had been built "to give racers full protection in the turns." The paper noted that "The circuit is planned to give the driver the best ride of his life and offers the spectators thrills, screeching of brakes, and flying rubber."

Sports writers noted that the turns were unbanked and constructed of various radii including a tough *chicane*, a hairpin bend, hard right-left, and three straights of more than 2/3rds miles. It was said that no course was tougher on cars as drivers had to hit the brakes and downshift no fewer than 19 times for each lap. Clutches, gearboxes, and brakes take a frightful beating.

Race creator Alec Ulmann earlier had broken his ties with the Sports Car Club of America, so the race was sanctioned by the American Automobile Association. Ulmann had worked a full year in getting the race listed on the international calendar, which would permit drivers from all over the world to compete in the event. Drivers were required to hold FIA licenses, and vehicles were limited to category-two sports cars. Ulmann also enlisted the help of Joe Lane as timer and scorer. It was Lane who suggested trophies for the overall winner—the longest distance covered, and FIA class cups in addition to the index of performance award.

Mrs. Zill Taylor Deshon (wife of the Sam Collier Memorial winner) was named to handle the press and public relations, Hemp Oliver was tapped as Chief Scrutineer (Automotive Tech Inspector) for the race, and Nils Mickelson again was the official starter.

Locally, Sebring Fire Chief Forrest Howard was the Race Chairman, Ford Heacock served as treasurer for the event, and Col. C.D. Richardson was selected as the program chairman.

The call also went out from L. Dean Mather, chairman of the scoring group, for 85 to 100 residents of Sebring and Highlands County to volunteer their services as scorers for the race. The system as set up would rotate individual scorers every two hours for the full 12-hour period. As an inducement, they offered a free meal to those who volunteered to serve.

Cypress Gardens creator, Dick Pope, reportedly sent his entire photographic crew to the event, and some of the competition was "televised to northern interests." Some of the journalists who were in attendance included Ken Purdy of *True Magazine,* Ben Kosivar, the associate editor of *Look,* Ogden Reed of the *New York Herald Tribune,* and Hy Peskin of *Time* & *Life*. Racers—both cars and drivers, were called in from all over the world.

As race day approached, the local newspaper chronicled the arrival of the competitors. Duke Donaldson had just come in with his Frazier-Nash *Le Mans* Formula racer aboard the *Queen Elizabeth*. They got there just in time so the car could be broken in by driver Harry Gray of England. Prophetically, the paper noted, "This is a car to watch during the 12-hour grind."

Also arriving via ship was René Bonnett, holder of eight French records. He and his crew, along with his Deutch Bonnet Panards, came to the Sunshine State aboard the *Il de France*.

The *Highlands County News* noted that Col. Richardson had flown to England to secure Sterling Moss, the British racing champion, to compete in the first 12-hour race. Moss had attained the highest aggregate score in 1951, most notably for his wins at Silverstone and *Le Mans*, plus the grand prix races in Holland and in Rome.

Both winners of the Sam Collier Grand Prix reported problems with their rides. Frits Koster had raced in Florida the previous week and developed engine problems with his Porsche. DeShon had mechanical difficulties with his Italian *Mille Miglia* but expected his parts to be shipped in by air so as to make the necessary repairs.

As area hotels filled to capacity, local residents began opening their homes to racers, officials, and media. This was the beginning of a great tradition in the early years.

Thirty-eight cars had qualified for the grid, however, only 32 vehicles actually started the race. Position in the starting line had been determined by drawing. Drivers again used the dramatic *Le Mans* type start, bolting across the home straightaway, jumping in their racers, and tearing off. As this was a sports car race, attempting to recreate a cross-country affair, drivers had to carry everything they needed for repairs onboard the car. Pit stops also were regulated to certain intervals, to simulate the driving space between towns, where one might find a service station with parts.

The *Highlands County News* reported the competition would run from noon to midnight, but heavy rain pushed the green flag back until that afternoon at 1:03 p.m. This was the one and only time the 12 Hours of Sebring had not been started at the advertised Western Union Time under creator Alec Ulmann. Due to the wet conditions, the North/South runway corner had to be changed, as there was a large puddle that refused to dry.

The weather was not the only thing the 1952 competition had to endure. Just the week before, the SCCA had put on a similar 12-hour race in Vero Beach. Although some drivers ran both competitions, others were damaged in the "2nd Annual Florida Handicap" at the Vero Beach Airport course and could not run at Sebring. Ken Breslaur's Sebring Record Book indicates the Cadillac Allard of Tommy Cole and Paul O'Shea, and the Ferrari of Jim Kimberly and Marshall Lewis were casualties of the Vero Beach affair.

There were only two leaders in the first 12 Hours of Sebring Grand Prix of Endurance. The winner was the *Le Mans* Replica Frazier-Nash, driven by Larry Kulok and Englishman Harry Gray. They overcame transmission problems to take the checkered flag. The Kulok/Gray team inherited the lead on the 51st lap when the Ferrari 340 of Briggs Cunningham and Bill Spear retired with differential problems. The Nash completed 145 laps, equaling 754 miles, for an average speed of 62.8 mph. Reportedly, by the end of the race, the winners had no clutch left.

1952 Sebring International Grand Prix of Endurance. The LeMans start shows drivers dashing for their cars. Reprinted with permission of the Sebring Historical Society.

The race is underway as cars jockey for position. Reprinted with permission of the Sebring Historical Society.

Only one American car finished, a Crosley Hot Shot driven by George Sanderson.

Published reports indicate there were some 7,000 fans in attendance at the race. Then-President Harry Truman was vacationing in the Florida Keys and was sent an invitation to join the throng, but apparently, he declined.

As in the Sam Collier Memorial, the guest of honor, Florida Governor Fuller Warren, handed out the trophies. The ceremonies were held the following day at Highlands Hammock State Park during an afternoon "Victory Barbecue." Those who wished could attend the all-you-can-eat luncheon for $1.50.

The "sportsmanship trophy" went to drivers Roger Wing and Steve Spitler who pushed their entry (a Morris) 4.5 miles to the pits after it developed engine trouble. The index of performance winner was the #25 Deutch-Bonnet. It is believed that René Bonnet drove the car along with Steve Lasing and Wade Morehouse. The Deutch-Bonnet racing effort was the first post World War II French team to compete in the United States.

Highlands County News columnist Jennie Reninger related a story of René Bonnet and his dedication to finishing the race.

"A few hours before the Grand Prix ended, one of the two cars refused to start after coming in to be refueled. I watched René Bonnct, and his brother remove and replace something from the innards of the car. They then started the machine by the tortuous method of jacking up the wheels and turning them by hand until the motor kicked over. Never during all that time did either man seem the least excited.

". . . when the engine finally fired, and the car went racing down the track . . . Never have I seen such exuberant rejoicing. The Frenchmen leaped into the air, waived their arms, shouted, and kissed everyone around."

Such is the stuff which built the mystique of the 12 Hours of Sebring.

Again, the Sebring Firemen staged the event and lost even more money on the deal than they did at the inaugural affair. Again, Col. Richardson picked up the tab. For his generosity, he was voted an honorary membership to the group.

The work involved for the men was arduous for at least a week ahead of time, and race day was described as "thoroughly exhausting"—all in a losing financial battle. The organization took a vote on whether or not to continue the race 'for one more year.' It passed by the slimmest of margins. It is conceded that a negative vote would have resulted in the end of 'The Race,' because most people believed that if the Sebring Firemen could not make it go, certainly nobody else could either. Also, the airport had sustained substantial damage and losses, and there was little chance that the management would look with favor on an operation in which the Firemen were not involved.

One of the factors that influenced the heavy negative vote was the miserable weather that followed the downpour which delayed the start of the race. It had been a balmy morning when the Firemen met at the airport to sweep the field of spectators who had come out earlier to hide under warehouses or in the tall grass to avoid paying admission prices. So they were totally unprepared for either the rain or the subsequent cold.

To compound the problem, there were not enough men to relieve those as flagmen, or who were on patrol in jeeps and on horseback, 'riding the rim' to keep spectators off the course (there were no fences at the time). So, by the midnight end of the race, they had nothing but unpleasant impressions. "At that hour, it would have been impossible to find a single vote in favor of a third race," said Altvader.

The race did pull in lots of favorable press, not the least of which was a four-page spread in *Look* magazine, with photos by Arthur Rothstein. It also was featured as the cover story of the August issue of *Motorsport* magazine.

Alec Ulmann returned to Sebring in April to address the local Lions Club. He was accompanied by Briggs Cunningham, who also brought one of his cars to test on the airport circuit in preparation for the 24-hour *Le Mans* race that would be held in June. At the session, Ulmann talked of the "joint advantages" of the 12-hour grand prix, both to the racing world and the Sebring community. The AAA already had sanctioned a race for 1953, but it had not been decided whether it would remain a 12-hour affair or become a 24-hour race like *Le Mans*.

This was not the only public appearance Ulmann would put in at Sebring in 1952; he returned in August to show movies of grand prix racing and to give details of next year's competition. It was to have a new name, "The Florida Grand Prix of Endurance." Ulmann also announced that he had placed a full-page ad in the

Le Mans program, talking about the 1953 race. Ulmann made headlines again in December when he popped into Sebring on a weekend visit with one of the nation's leading stock car promoters—Jake Kedenburg of New York and Tampa. Ulmann told reporters that the field for 1953 would be limited to 60 cars and predicted a record crowd for the race.

1953—The Grand Prix of Endurance

The 1953 Sebring race ran on March 8 and carried the moniker "The Florida International Grand Prix of Endurance."

The event now had been sanctioned by the FIA and carried the distinction as one of the World Manufacturer's Championship Endurance Races. The series had been initiated earlier that year by the Commission Sportive International. This meant the competition counted toward World Cup points. No other race in America shared that honor.

When Ulmann received the cable from France, he wasted no time in sharing the news with local newspapers and radio.

The 12 Hours of Sebring and the Indianapolis 500 Sweepstakes were the only American races listed on the

The pit area still pretty spartan for competitors in the 1953 12-Hours of Sebring. (Doug Morton Collection)

Auto Sporting Calendar of the World. The FIA points put Sebring on a par with such races as *Le Mans* in France, the Tourist Trophy of England, the Pan American Road Race in Mexico, and the famous *Mille Miglia* of Italy.

Shell Oil furnished the gas and oil for the race, marking the first petroleum company to recognize Sebring. In addition to a plentiful amount of premiums such as posters, cups and the like, Shell also provided a giant banner to be stretched above the start/finish line. The company embarked on a massive advertising campaign for the second around-the-clock competition, and, as part of the deal, drivers would run for the overall win—to be known as "The Sebring Shell Cup."

It was through the auspices of Shell that Alec Ulmann was able to enlist the duties of George E.T. Eyeston as the official starter. And, says Ulmann, "Eyeston did more than simply wave the flag—his knowledge of course protection helped officials to mark the layout through the prudent placement of hay bales and other circuit markers." Eyeston was best known for his conquest of the world land speed record and had been dubbed "the 357-mph man." He also was a trained engineer, and a member of the board of the Castrol Oil Company.

There were other notables serving as race officials. S. Hempstone Oliver returned. He served as Chief inspector. Oliver was the Curator of Transportation at the Smithsonian Institute in Washington D.C. Chief Scrutineer Dean Fales who had been Ulmann's professor of automotive engineering at the Massachusetts Institute of Technology also was selected to serve.

Officials were listed as:
- Alec Ulmann—Chief Steward
- Reginald Smith—secretary
- Joseph Lane—Chief Server
- Fred Asche—Pit steward

The race committee consisted of:
- Forrest Howard—General Chairman
- Ford Heacock—co-chairman
- Col. C.D. Richardson co-chairman
- J.M. McAdams
- Frank Bryant
- Tom Dimberline
- Allen C. Altvader
- Jim Fulton

Apparently, the reputation of the race was growing quickly. As early as February 20, there was an article in the *Highlands County News* that hotels in the area already were being swamped for reservations. The *Avon Park Sun* also encouraged residents there with rooms to rent to contact the Sebring Chamber of Commerce, as the city was "jammed with an influx of people to see the car races."

As in the previous year, there was another SCCA sports car race run just prior to the 12 Hours. This one was the "Florida National Sports Car Race" which was held at MacDill Airfield in the Tampa area the week before. Proceeds of that 500-mile event were used to improve the living conditions of the airmen stationed there. Newspaper reports projected that "thousands of fans" who witnessed that event would now come to Sebring.

Promoters hoped that the popularity of the Sebring contest might also encourage local fans to travel to Tampa for their competition, and advance tickets were made available at the Avon Park Chamber of Commerce. Those who purchased the pre-sale tickets also would be eligible to win the gate prize—a new automobile.

Possibly, the greatest news of that year for Sebring was word that the famous English Aston Martin team would join the French factory DB's for the 12 Hour competition. In fact, David Brown, the head of the British auto firm, came over to watch the race.

Ulmann believed that the entry by René Bonnet's DB Pannards the previous year had done a great deal to spur that kind of effort, both in the caliber of race teams, and in the image presented to the FIA's Commission Sportive headed by Monsieur Perouse. Part of Aston Martin's participation may have come from Jack Law. He was a P.R. man for the auto maker, and a former officer who had served at Hendricks Field during the war years.

There also had been an announcement in December 1952 that the people of Le Mans, France, would try to field a team of cars for this race. It was to be a means to show their appreciation for the visits of Briggs Cunningham and his team to their most famous of road races.

The plan had been to sell subscriptions and with the assistance of sportsmen and racing enthusiasts they would send a trio of vehicles, to be piloted by amateur drivers. The effort was spearheaded by the "Sporting Automobile

Club of Le Mans," with the blessing of the Governor of the Department of the Sarthe, Lord Mayor and the Le Mans Chamber of Commerce. Unfortunately, it does not appear that the effort was too successful, and there is no indication that they ever ran at Sebring.

Many faces were starting to become familiar; it was announced that among the returning car owners and drivers there would be Duke Donaldson, René Bonnet, Luigi Chinetti, René Dryfus, Jim Kimberly, and Stirling Moss. Briggs Cunningham and Briggs Cunningham III became the first father/son team to drive the race.

Practice runs were held Thursday and Friday. Fans were allowed into the track on Friday "for a small admission charge."

The race was run from noon until midnight, on a day described as "partly cloudy and mild."

An estimated 12,500 fans showed up for the race—a sharp increase over the year before. As security, ten additional Miami Police officers had been brought in to aid the local men who managed crowd control duties. Also assisting was the American Legion Reserve Police Unit of Highlands Post 69, who enthusiastically responded to the call from Sheriff Broward Coker. They were joined by Miami Legionaries from Post 25, recognized as the best trained and organized unit of its kind.

Later, Captain Barney of the Miami Police Department would remark that the crowd was the most polite and cooperative with which he had ever worked.

The Aston Martins made a good showing, leading the first 32 laps of the race before retiring as a result of an accident. The #57 Cunningham CR4 then took the point and was never bested.

For the second time, the winner was an American car. In fact, the Cunningham was a Florida-made car, and one of only American contenders. Ironically, the car had been entered for the race the previous year but was withdrawn because it was not yet ready for competition.

Powered by a 542cc Chrysler engine, the Cunningham had been fabricated in West Palm Beach and was a street legal automobile. In fact, it ran the 12 Hours carrying a Florida license plate.

The car was driven by John Fitch and Phil Walters— the General Manager of the West Palm Beach racing plant. They were boosted to the lead when the front-running Aston Martin of Geoff Duke and Peter Collins collided with a Jaguar and was eliminated at the three-hour mark.

Fitch and Walters won by a lap over one of the Aston Martin DB3's. The Reg Parnell/George Abecassis entry reportedly was hampered by the fact that one of its headlamps did not work.

There was one car fire; the Cadillac Allard of Paul Ramos was destroyed when a fuel line broke. However, driver Anthony Cumming escaped unharmed. Another competitor, Randy Pearsall, escaped injury when his Jaguar XK 120 flipped. There was quite a bit of attrition—of the 55 cars that started the race, only 35 finished.

The winning drivers received stop watches from the Champion Spark Plug Company. In addition to the Sebring Shell Trophy, the Cunningham team also took the Cop-Si-Loy Award.

The Aston Martin team won both the Marchal Trophy for best overall performance, and the KLG-Nisonger award for pit efficiency.

Dick Irish of Cleveland was the winner of the Shell Oil Sportsmanship Trophy. His Excalibur burned up its differential and he pushed the vehicle two miles to the pit.

The Deutch-Bonnet of Wade Moorehouse and René Bonnett was the index of performance winner for the second year in a row. An important step forward that year had been the adoption of what promoter Alec Ulmann termed "a far more satisfactory index of performance." It was the creation of Timing & Scoring Chief Joe Lane, with more emphasis placed on the winners' distance.

1954—A Historic Upset

In his book, *The Sebring Story*, Ulmann says that the officials from Shell Oil went so far over their budget in sponsoring the race in 1953 that they dropped out of such programs for quite some time.

However, American Oil Company stepped in the following year to fill the gap. As part of the arrangement, competitors would be furnished with Amoco gasoline as the official and only fuel used for the 12-hour endurance classic.

Alec Ulmann brought several AMOCO officials to Sebring in February of 1954, prior to the race. They included Glen Alsup, the Florida Sales Manager based in Jacksonville, Advertising Manager for AMOCO Oil, E. F. Kalkhof, and R. G. Swan, the Vice President of the Swartz Agency of New York.

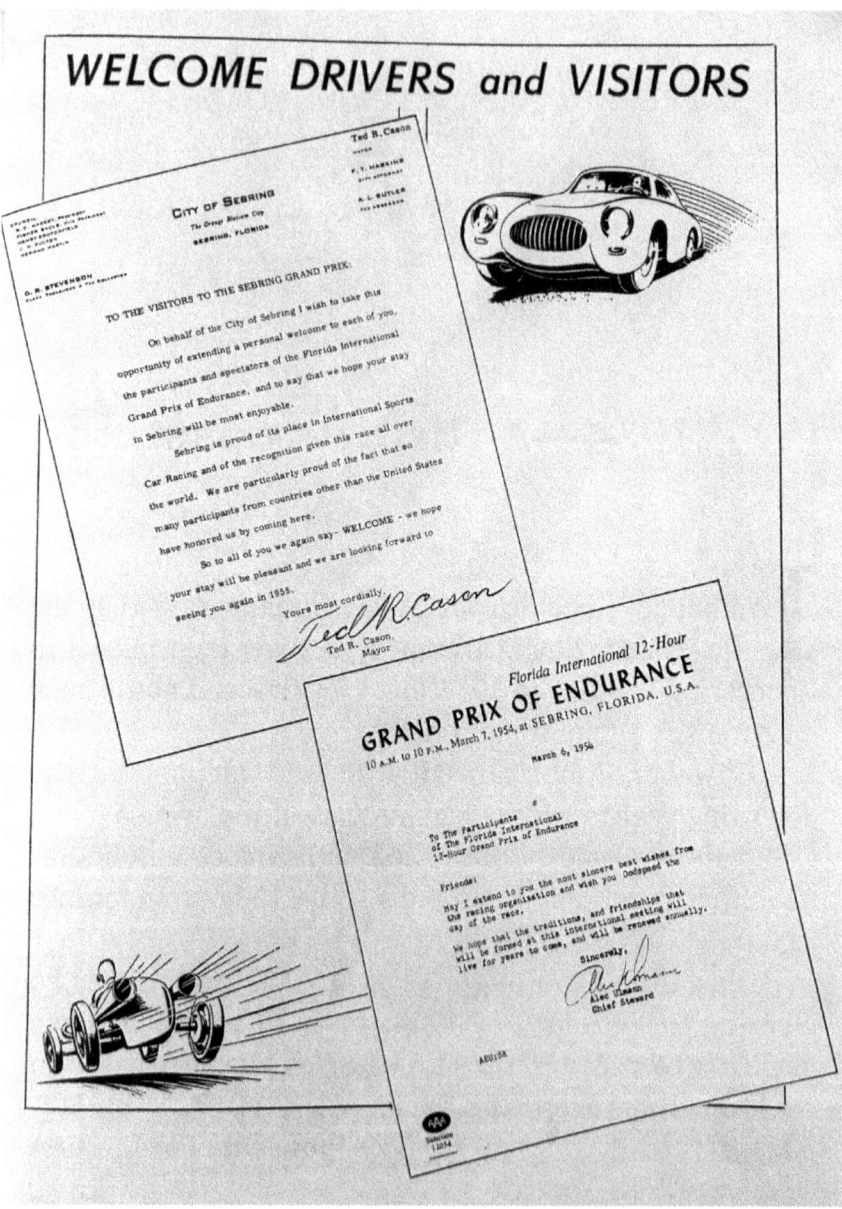

Fans who bought programs were greeted with twin welcome letters from race creator Alec Ulmann and Sebring Mayor Ted Cason. Reprinted with permission of the Sebring Historical Society.

The trio was pleased with the prospect of spending some time in Sebring and were looking forward to their return in March for the race.

Publicity about the competition was made available to visitors, with folders distributed in welcome stations at Yulee, Jay, Hilliard, Jennings, Campbellton, and Pensacola through the information service of the State Road Department.

Apparently, it worked, by mid-February the calls for accommodations were already being sounded. Newspaper reports said that local hotels, motels, and other rooming establishments were booked solid, and requests still were being received. The Sebring Firemen's Accommodations Committee and the Chamber of Commerce Housing Committee appealed to citizens of Avon Park, Sebring, and Lake Placid to make available rooms in their homes to visitors of the race—noting that many were willing to pay hotel rates.

A billboard announcing the 1954 12-Hour race was planted on the Circle in downtown Sebring. Reprinted with permission of the Sebring Historical Society.

In 1954, organizers also began adding to the atmosphere of the race. They started by naming a race queen. The announcement of that competition came in January, with applications to obtained at the Hotel Sebring.

Sue Gillen of Lake Wales was the first one selected.

Her official title—"The International Queen of Speed." Her majesty's official duties were to reign "over the race and pre-race festivities" as well as to represent the "pretty wives and sweethearts of the famous sports car drivers and manufacturers from all over the world . . ."

For her efforts, the Florida Southern College Drama-Voice major won a number of prizes from local merchants. They included a three-piece set of luggage from Kahn's Department Store, a swimsuit from Fremac's, a permanent wave from Milady's Salon, a photo session with *Highlands County News* photographer, Jesse Woods, a tropical handbag from the Woodrose Shop, and a set of pearls from Jackson Jewelry.

At least one local veteran's group saw the fund-raising possibilities of the race, as Post 69 of the American Legion set up a food booth. The Legion's auxiliary also helped in that effort.

Meanwhile, Alec Ulmann's worldwide travel was lining up notables from all over the globe. Among the visiting dignitaries were Lord & Lady Lascelles, cousin to Queen Elizabeth, and Gar Wood, the former speedboat king, among others.

The Aston Martin factory effort announced in February that they would compete in the Sebring endurance race. The *Avon Park Sun* reported at the time that the cars were

Cars and drivers came from all over the world to compete at Sebring. Publicist Reggie Smith highlighted that fact with this map from the **1954 Race Headquarters**, outlining where entrants had traveled to arrive for the test at Sebring. (Bill Foster Collection)

in Argentina, competing in Buenos Aires, but would be shipped by boat to New Orleans, then trucked to central Florida.

They were the first European entry to be announced.

A unique plan that year called for the Sebring Race Committee to name two top American drivers to run one of the Aston Martin team racers. They did, however, require that ". . . the nominees be both capable of and have enough experience to drive these fast cars."

Famous designer of sports cars, Donald Healy, was tapped as the official starter of the 1954 Sebring Grand Prix. Once a successful driver in British and international circles, Healy now was better known as the creator of the Austin Healy which had been displayed at the 12 Hour race in 1952.

Healy also was known for other hybrids. In 1948, he built his "dream car," the Healy (his namesake) which won the famous Italian *Mille Migla*; then in 1950, he collaborated with the American Nash company in the development of the Nash-Healy. One of his cars also was entered in the 1954 race.

Some of that year's race participants who also were noted in other fields of endeavor included ex-congressman Jim Simpson (he finished third), "international playboy" Porfirio Rubirosa—then the newest husband of Barbra (Babs) Hutton, and the Marquis de Portago—a well-known equestrian and the ranking Spanish nobility at the time.

The race headquarters downtown was given "a Florida touch" as it was decorated by the Sebring Garden Club with tropical and sub-tropical flowers. Local packers also chipped in by donating citrus so that visitors "could help themselves."

That was a theme that later would be repeated at the raceway. Highlands County News columnist, Jennie Reninger, noted that orange baskets had replaced hay bales as track markers, and . . . "In front of the pits are baskets of free oranges for the benefit of drivers and mechanics."

In an attempt to handle the hungry throng when race week came, the PTA cafeteria at the Sebring High

School was opened over the weekend. During selected hours, interested people had their choice of baked ham or chicken dinners.

In one of his accounts, Reuters correspondent Hayden Williams noted:

"Thousands of spectators are expected to line the 5.2-mile road course at Hendricks Field to see the speed demons in their sleek, low-slung cars roaring over the runways and streets of the deactivated Air Force base for 12 hours . . ." Further, he promised ". . . there will be thrills galore for the sports car fans on the dangerous turns of the course as the drivers come to them, many after hitting speeds of 135 mph on the straightaways."

The Publicity officers of the AAA Contest Board were advised that because of the entries of so many famous international drivers, owners, and spectators, updates from the race would be beamed behind the Iron Curtain through the services of the Voice of America. The race winners also would receive a 10-minute radio interview.

In all, some 14,000 fans turned out on that sunny and cool March 7 to watch one of the most exciting races to date. To help manage the additional traffic created by the crowd, Highlands County Sheriff Broward Coker arranged with Captain Jim Barney of the Miami Auxiliary Police (American Legionaries) to have 35 members assigned to Sebring. The Florida Highway Patrol also allocated extra troopers. First Aid duties were handled by the Red Cross, and two ambulances were stationed at the track for the affair.

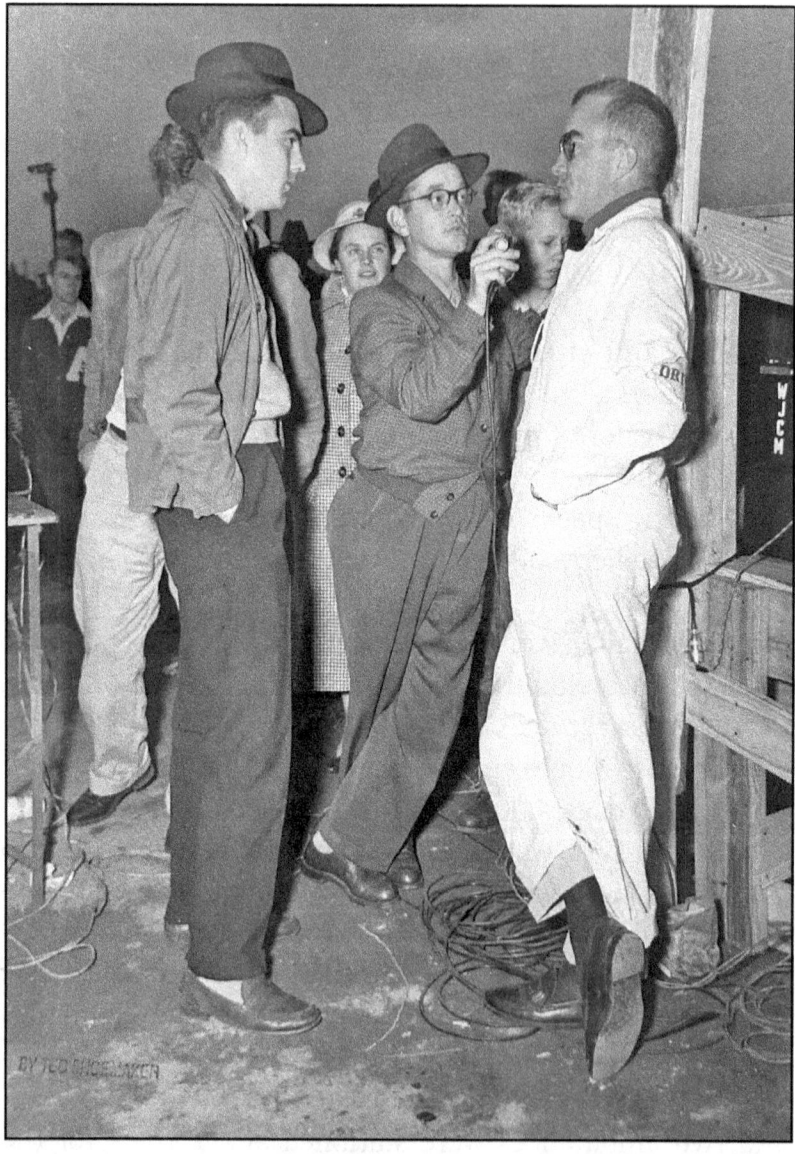

Local radio station WJCM had announcers **Al Frank** and **Ron Wilson** out talking with drivers, officials, and other principals of the race. Reprinted with permission of the Sebring Historical Society.

The starting time for the race was moved to 10 a.m., to accommodate newspaper deadlines. There were 59 cars that started the race, but only 25 finished.

The 1954 competition had one of the strangest entries in Sebring's history—a car called the Rex. It was driven by William Wood and was powered by a Mercury outboard motor. The unusual machine failed inspection, and did not qualify.

The Lancia entries, as expected, were the class of the field. They dominated most of the day.

During the early going, it was the entries of Juan Fangio/Eugenio Castelotti and Albert Ascari & Gigi Villoresi who swapped the lead back and forth. The Ferrari 375 of Phil Hill & Bill Spear had a run at the front, but finally relinquished the point to the Lancia of "The Gray Fox" Piero Taruffi/Robert Manzon who then led for more than one hundred laps.

But at Sebring, the race does not always belong to the fastest, but rather the most reliable cars. One by one, the Lancias fell by the wayside, experiencing a myriad of different problems over the long, rough surface of the racetrack. The last of them finally gave way with just seven laps to go. Published reports say Taruffi pushed the car two miles back to the pits, only to be disqualified because the car did not finish under its own power.

The race was won by Englishman Stirling Moss and William Lloyd of Green Farms, Connecticut, who were driving the Briggs Cunningham-prepared OSCA.

The win by the OSCA has been termed "one of the biggest upsets in endurance racing."

Here we see the 1954 Lancia team unloading one of their race cars at the Stiles-Johnson Pontiac Dealership on South Commerce Street in downtown Sebring. They had rented the garage to work on the car during race week. During the early days of the race, many teams used auto dealerships, service stations and other garages in the area to work on their vehicles, which then were driven to the airport to compete. (Bill Foster Collection)

In addition to their fleet of racers, in 1954, the Lancia team arrived with a number of "official cars," to be used for local transportation for their drivers, team members and principals. (Bill Foster Collection)

Reportedly, fans were treated to a fireworks display at the end of the competition.

No money was awarded, but there were plenty of trophies. Winners Sterling Moss and his co-driver William Lloyd walked away with the lion's share—taking the French Auto Club du Var award, the Auto Age trophy, and the Nisonger K-L-G trophy for winning the index of performance.

The Tom Cole Award given by Ferrari went to Briggs Cunningham, owner of the OSCA. OSCA representative Edgar Fronteras accepted the *Car Life* "Award of Merit," on behalf of the team for their best performance.

The Dunlop Tire "Gold Cup" for sportsmanship went to the Aston Martin Co. and drivers Bill Carpenter and Jack van Dreil took the Donald Healy Trophy for their performance in the Kieft-Bristol. That honor was presented to the best finish by Americans in a British-made car. They came in 5th overall.

Although there were no fatalities during the race, the *Highlands County News* noted that 39-year-old James Brundage, a former competitor, died in Ft. Lauderdale on his way back to his home in Miami. At 3:30 Sunday morning, the Allard he was driving hit a tree.

The Sebring Chamber of Commerce estimated that the local economy realized nearly $3,000.00 in benefits to business from the race. Later reports indicated the race itself made nearly that much, netting $2,937.53 in profits.

The Sebring Jaycees were not happy about the *Tampa Tribune's* reporting of the event—or, the lack of it. On the front page of the April 2 edition of the *Highlands County*

News, they published a resolution saying they would boycott the *'Tribune'* for its inadequate coverage of the international competition.

There also was some fallout for running the race on Sunday. *The Highlands County News* carried letters on successive weeks from citizens Effa B. Hicks and Clinton Ganse who wholeheartedly supported the Sebring Firemen's efforts—and just as adamantly opposed running such an event on the Sabbath.

An April 30 article revealed what was to become another common theme over the coming years—improvements at the track. "To ensure sanctioning of future races," the AAA had requested that the race promoters make a number of changes including the sheltering of the pits, and the fencing in of spectator areas.

Before the year was out, the 'Race' was to have another accolade. The Fraser-Nash company named a car model "Sebring." It was the company's custom to name a car after the town in which the car had been a winner.

A Fraser-Nash, of course, had taken the checkers in the very first 12-hour endurance grand prix at the air terminal.

Not long after the race, a founder of the event, Miles Collier, succumbed to polio. He had returned to racing with a small Bandini, hoping to take part in major races. The 25,000 in attendance for the '1954 12 Hours' had shown that interest in European style road racing that he and his brother had helped nurture, really was taking hold in America.

1955—A Truly International Race

The 1955 season was the 5th running of the "Florida Grand Prix of Endurance."

The General Chairman of the Race Committee, Ford Heacock, apparently in response to concerns expressed the year before by the AAA, announced the first major improvements to the track in a speech to the Sebring Lions Club in February of that year.

The 5.2-mile course had been widened and smoothed in several places, "with new asphalt toppings." This was for safety, and would allow the cars to achieve greater speed, especially in some of the corners. Eighty individual pits had been installed down the front straightaway, along with a permanent judges and timer's stand made of concrete block.

Another innovation would be cardboard course markers—replacing the former orange basket and sand-filled oil drum-type markers. There was to be over a mile of "snow fence" erected from the curve at the start of the home stretch to the airport offices as a safeguard to keep fans from getting onto the track. The former blackboard method of keeping spectators advised of the race standings had been supplanted by the addition of a new aluminum scoreboard. But the greatest addition was the construction of a 60-foot-long steel suspension bridge. Installed over the start/finish line; it would aid those wishing to traverse into the pit area. This was a great hit with the public, and they were happy to pay to use the new span which would bear the Amoco advertising logo for five years.

In 1955, the first "tower" was built at the raceway. It remains unclear if this was used for scoring, for radio broadcast, or some kind of official function. (Bill Foster Collection)

A canvas start/finish banner had hung in the same location for the 1953 and 1954 races.

The date of the race also had been changed; it was pushed back from March 20 to March 13. The idea was to avoid the rain—and records indicate that in Florida, March is the driest month of the year. A decade later, there would be an exception to the rule.

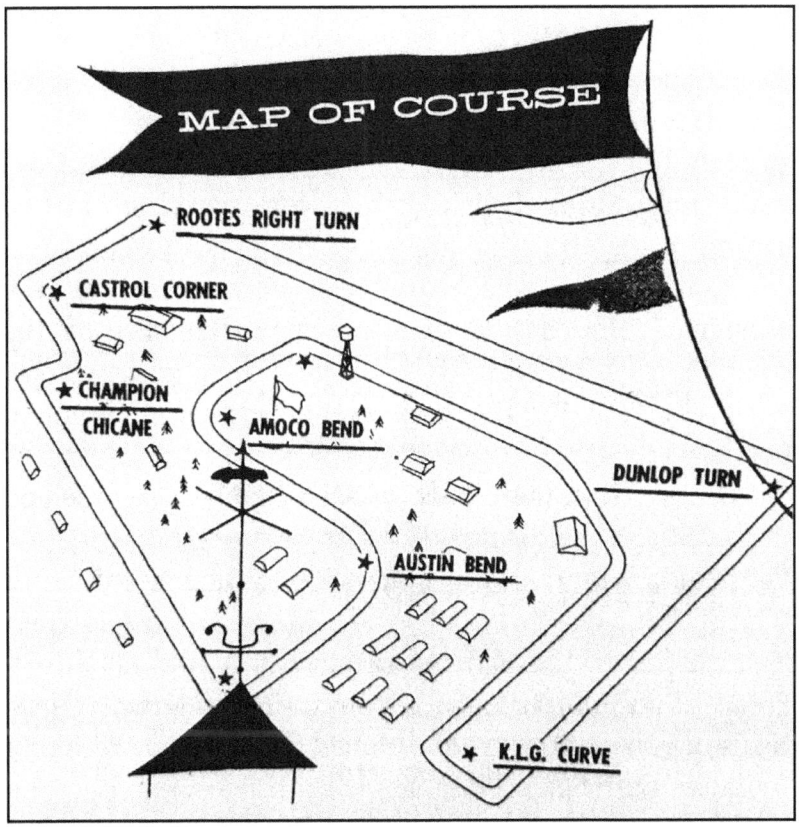

By 1955, they had named parts of the raceway in honor of some of the sponsors. Reprinted with permission of the Sebring Historical Society.

By 1955, the 12 Hours of Sebring began to blossom as a recognized international affair. Race Secretary Reginald Smith told news reporters from his headquarters in the Sebring Hotel that "This year's response to the special invitational meeting exceeds anything we have ever experienced," and that "the eyes of the world" were on Sebring.

Indeed, the call for rooms to rent from the Sebring Chamber of Commerce had gone out in the year's first edition of the *Highlands County News*. By mid-January, 600 requests for lodging had been received, and "more are arriving each day." Local officials conceded that surrounding towns would be called upon to house the many international visitors but were working hard to centralize the economic impact in Highlands County.

Again, there would be plenty of hardware for the race winners. Promoters took the opportunity to show off the trophies, trays, and awards, by placing them in the display window of The Kiddie Shop on the Circle, in downtown Sebring.

By race time, there were a dozen countries represented in the 80-car field, including the first go-round for the Venezuelan team. They had 1954 champion Chester "Chet" Flynn leading that effort. Mexico also had their first entries in the Sebring race, with a two-car effort. Fred T. Van Beuren and Carlos Braniff were their pilots. Not since the 1952 Olympic games had so many different countries participated in a single sporting event.

The race saw the entry of its first Hollywood film star as Jackie Cooper, who signed on with Roy Moore and

Jackie Cooper becomes the first Hollywood star to race at Sebring. He piloted this Austin-Healey. Reprinted with permission of the Sebring Historical Society.

drove an Austin-Healy 100S. Miss Isabel Haskell of New Jersey was to become the first woman to compete not only in the 12 Hours of Sebring—but in any AAA sanctioned racing event. Although the AAA did not allow women race car drivers, Haskell apparently discovered that there was no such prohibition in foreign races. Haskell announced she planned to drive for a foreign team. So, by race time, the "girl from New Jersey" had residence in Andover, England, and Palm Beach.

Described in local news accounts as a "wheelwoman," Haskell was scheduled to drive an 1100cc Bandini, but records place her behind the wheel of a Siata Fiat with Clevelander Dick Irish. Another woman also ultimately signed on to drive in the race, Lady Greta Oakes, took the wheel with her Bahama-based British industrialist husband, Sir Sidney Oakes. Although Cooper managed to finish the race, the Haskell/Irish entry did not. They went out with an apparent engine malfunction. The Oakes' Austin-Healy also drew a DNF when they were involved in an accident.

There also was a trio of entrants to try the Grand Prix who were known for their driving in another famous race, the Indianapolis 500. They included Jim Rathman of Miami, Jim Hanks of Burbank, California, and Cal Niday of Los Angeles, California. Rathman and Ensley were paired in a Kurtis 500 while Niday would join Dominican sportsmen, Porfirio Rubirosa, in a Mondial Ferrari. In the end, neither paring had an auspicious debut. The Rubirosa/Niday entry finished 71st overall, when Rubirosa spun out and badly damaged the car early in the race. The Ensley/Rathman entry completed only three laps when engine problems forced their Kurtis to retire.

There was a fourth Indy driver scheduled to compete. Ray Crawford of Elmonte, California, was scheduled to drive a Lincoln-Kurtis Special at the 12 Hours. He would debut at the brickyard later that same year.

Returning for another go-round were Americans Phil Hill and Carroll Shelby, German Baron von Hanstein, Frenchman René Dryfus, Spain's Marques de Portago, and British champion, Stirling Moss. Moss, who piloted the OSCA to victory the previous year, would take over the driving duties of Donald Healy in a 100S with fellow Brit, Lance Macklin. Moss also brought another of his countrymen for a taste of the 12 Hours—Mike Hawthorne.

Although Hawthorne had been associated for many years with the Ferrari racing teams, He would drive the new D-Jaguar.

Advertisements billed the competition as "Testing skill and stamina in a 12-hour thrill-packed race"—and all for a two-dollar spectator admission fee.

In addition to well-known drivers, press releases touted the new cars that would be taking to the track in the world class competition. Briggs Cunningham was returning with a new C-6R; the D-type Jag, and owner/driver Fred Scherer of Skokie, Illinois, was to put the new Ford Thunderbird into the competition.

Accounts noted that Cunningham's entry was "still under wraps," but that "the cream of the European automotive industry" would have their eye on the performance of the T-Bird. Another American entrant brought his creation—owner/designer Brooks Stevens drove his Excalibur in the race.

There were two days of practice before the '12 Hours' and the 1955 race saw the advent of the first nighttime practice on the course.

Papers also make mention of a cocktail party thrown at Harder Hall as a pre-race feature. Films of previous Sebring races, and the Pan-American race were shown as entertainment.

An estimated 20,000 spectators showed up on a warm and sunny March 13. The Sebring Boy Scouts hoisted the flags of the individual nations in opening ceremonies, while the Palm Beach Air Force Band played the national anthems of each country involved.

It was Florida Senator George A. Smathers who secured the services of the Air Force's band. He made the request ". . . due to the international aspect of the race . . ."

In his account of the action, Hayden Williams wrote ". . . the thousands who witnessed the grueling race will ever remember the battle between the Jaguar and the Ferrari." Statistics show that the D-type Jaguar led all but one of the 182 completed laps. Early in the competition, a Ferrari 750S Monza driven by Piero Taruffi & Harry Schell was able to take to the front for lap 32.

There were no fatalities or serious injuries in the race. However, one Ferrari fell prey to fire, another spun into an ambulance of the Draper Funeral Home damaging both vehicles. Briggs Cunningham's highly touted C-6R did not finish; the car broke a crankshaft. The race itself ended in confusion. At one point, the Ferrari was declared the winner, then it was the D-type Jaguar. The Jag was called to the winner's circle but had run out of gas during the victory lap. Luigi Chinetti, the Ferrari representative from New York (and former winner of the *LeMans 24*), protested the finish which was counter-protested by Jaguar owner Briggs Cunningham. Cunningham insisted that the Jag had passed the Ferrari. Ferrari owner Allen Guiberson, a Texas oilman, demanded that the D-type be disqualified on the grounds that it had overtaken the Ferrari under a yellow flag. Cunningham countered that the index of performance trophy had been given in error to the Hill/

Shelby Ferrari, when in fact, it should have gone to the OSCA driven by Bill Lloyd and George Huntoon.

The AAA contest board called a meeting March 21 at the Commodore Hotel in New York City to make a final decision. They inspected the records of Guiberson, Cunningham, and Timer Joe Lane. The four-man group headed by Acting Chairman Stewart Smyth declared the Jaguar the winner by ten seconds. Cunningham's protest was disallowed, and the Ferrari was ruled the handicap winner under the index of performance.

This was due in part to an admission by Ferrari team chief Ugolini that he had forgotten to count a lap. Thus, Phil Walters became the first driver to win the Grand Prix of Endurance twice, having co-driven the Cunningham CR4 through the checkers with John Fitch in the 1952 race.

In a race week issue of the *Highlands County News*, there was a poem written under the pseudonym Anthra Cite entitled "Meaning of the Grand Prix,"

> The Grand Prix of Endurance means:
> Sebring bulging at the seams
> Thousands of visitors
> Clean cut men—and women—in search of
>   honors
> Sportsmanship is the byword
> Flags of many nations
> Pennants waving in the breeze

Sporty—and costly—cars with their deep throated rumbling as they leave the city for the course
Race headquarters at the Hotel Sebring, a modern tower of Babel
Hearing French, German, Spanish, Italian, English of the British and American
Speed, speed and more speed being developed in the practice runs
Hotels, motels, trailer parks, rooming houses, private homes filled
Cash registers jingling with the influx of the sports car clan
Famous names in sports car circles
Boon in telephone and telegraph business
World-wide publicity for Sebring by pictures, radio, television, and the written word
Reporters sending the race news around the globe
Magazine writers with their colorful stories
Alec Ulmann, *major domo* of the Grand Prix
Reggie Smith, man of action with details big and small
Car manufacturers with an eye on the outcome
Seeing a grand bunch of fellows

If there was any doubt that the name of Sebring was being carried around the globe, evidence was presented in June, when a local boy stationed in Germany informed the *Highlands County News,* that a "Little Sebring" race had been staged by the Hesse Motor Sports Club in Landstuhl, Germany.

The competition was run on a 3.9-mile course, which had been laid out on an unused airfield.

Pvt. Alton Harnage said he also had seen newsreel footage of the Sebring races, and ". . . became homesick when he recognized Bucky Kahn cavorting around the track."

Sanctioning for the 1956 race already had been announced, and by September, B.C. "Bun" Perkins, chairman of the concessions committee for the 1956 race, already was calling on all civic, fraternal, and military organizations planning to seek concession space to contact him as soon as possible.

Alfred Momo, a famous automotive expert, inspects clean engine parts of torn down Maserati after 1955 Sebring race. Reprinted with permission of the Sebring Historical Society.

1956—The ARCF Emerges

The 1956 season brought new twists to the race. It began in the summer of 1955 with a tragedy at *Le Mans*. Eighty fans were killed when a car ran into the crowd and exploded. The AAA, the major sanctioning body in the United States, pulled out of racing events, leaving Sebring without an official sanction.

So, Alec Ulmann formed a new sanctioning body—The Automobile Racing Club of Florida (ARCF), with himself as president and Reggie Smith as vice president. Ulmann convinced the FIA that the group would make sure that all participants had international licenses.

The **Auto Racing Club of Florida** was created to sanction the '12 Hours' in 1955. Reprinted with permission of the Sebring Historical Society.

For the first time, cash prizes would be offered—$10,000 in all. Some officials had worried that might exclude some Sports Car Club of America drivers, who were amateurs in the truest sense of the word. However, in February of the year, the SCCA president, Jim Kimberly, issued a statement saying his board would allow drivers to compete, with the proviso that they sign a wavier agreeing not to accept any of the prize monies.

The Federation International l'Automobile (FIA) had limited the field to 60 entries. By race day, there were quite a few competitors signed on in search of prize money and world sports car title points. World Champion Manuel Fangio of Argentina led the Ferrari contingent. Jaguar announced they would return to Sebring with a works team of no fewer than five D-Types. The effort would be headed by defending champions Mike Hawthorne and Phil Walters. Briggs Cunningham was tapped to direct the team. That would position him to seek a fourth consecutive win as a car owner. American Champion Bob Sweikert would wheel a sixth, privately entered D-type Jaguar. Sweikert had won the prestigious Indianapolis 500 the year before, was the Midwest Sprint Car champion, and the current national point leader. It was his first time in a road race.

Sweikert would be joined on the grid by two other American champions—American amateur king, Sherwood Johnston, who also ran a Jaguar D, and 1952 Indy 500 winner, Troy Ruttman, who wheeled a Ferrari. The Cubans entered the fray for the first time with their champion, Santiago Gonzales in a Jaguar D. Spanish driving leader the Marquis Alfonso de Portago would drive a Ferrari,

Italian Champion Eugenio Castelotti shared the Ferrari ride with Fangio, and English racing titlist and former Sebring winner, Stirling Moss, who drove an Aston Martin DB3S. It also was the first year for an American factory entry, as four Corvettes were placed on the grid. Three of them ran in the stock "C" class, while one, with a larger-displacement engine, was moved up into the tougher "B" division.

Veteran Sebring racers, John Fitch and George Huntoon, began testing the vehicles on the racecourse in early February. But in a subsequent magazine article, Fitch would reveal just how far behind the Europeans the American manufacturers were in this type of competition.

Actually, a Corvette had first been entered in the race back in 1954, when F. F. Young Jr. of West Palm Beach had signed on to race. There was quite a bit of speculation on how ". . . the plastic body car . . . would fare in the around-the-clock grind."

But despite being accepted by the screening committee the car was withdrawn, and did not start the competition.

Of the 60 cars, there were 14 factory entries, and 10 nations represented. The Maserati team entered three cars, as did Ferrari, who enlisted Fangio in an attempt to win back the world manufacturing title. Mercedes Benz had captured it . . . but they had pulled out of racing after the tragedy at *Le Mans*. The Maseratis already had a jump on the competition, winning the first race on the seven-stop FIA calendar at Buenos Aires, Argentina. Sebring was to be the second date on the tour. The date also had to be pushed back from the previously announced March 25.

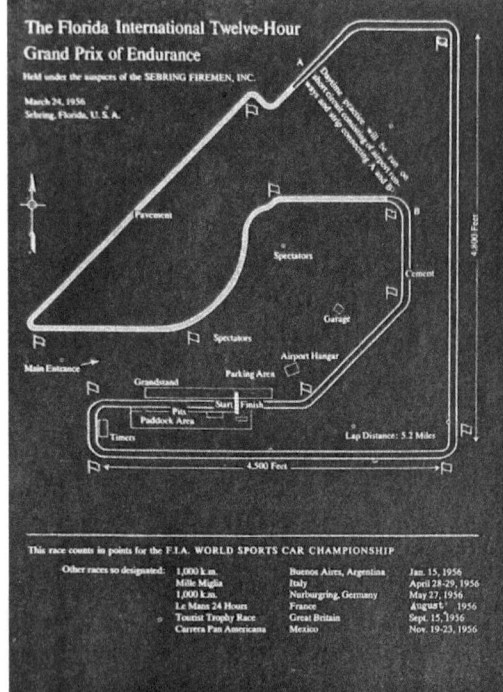

The Florida International Twelve-Hour Grand Prix of Endurance

March 24, 1956
Sebring, Florida, U. S. A.

Held under the auspices of the SEBRING FIREMEN, INC., Member of the *Association Internationale des Circuits Permanents*, Paris, France.

Registered on the International Calendar of the Federation Internationale de l'Automobile and held under its Sporting Code and the Supplementary Regulations provided hereunder and sanctioned by the Federation Internationale de l'Automobile,
    Appointed by the Federation Internationale de l'Automobile to constitute the sole United States event to count for point awards towards the World Sports Car Championship during the year 1956.

SEBRING RACE COMMITTEE

Allen C. Altvater	W. W. Harshman
Frank Bryant	James Fulton
Ford W. Heacock	Ray Morgan
J. W. McAdams	Dallas Durrance
Forrest Howard	Kenneth Wilson
Broward Coker	Wm. C. Schaeffer
Beau Brummell	Dr. Seron
Al Munson	C. B. Carter
Miles Baker	Dale Miller
C. C. Rutland	Robert Butts
Bill Sebring	B. C. Perkins
Sidney Cooper	

RACE OFFICIALS

Clerk of the Course	Alec E. Ulmann
Race Secretary	Reginald Smith
Chief Race Steward	William J. Smyth
Race Steward	John Baus
Race Steward	Robert Sturnpf
Judge of Facts	Prof. Dean A. Fales
Chief Scorer and Timer	Joseph J. Lane
Chief Pit Steward	Frederick T. Royston
Chief Scrutineer	Monty Thomas
Medical Director	A. J. Mirkin, MD, FACS
Starter	Henry Woeller
Trophy Chairman	Mary F. Ulmann
Reception Chairman	Frankie Watts

OPERATING COMMITTEE - F.I.A.
Reginald S. Smith
John Baus
Frederick Royston

Reprinted with permission of the Sebring Historical Society.

As that was Palm Sunday, the race was moved back to Saturday, March 24.

Again, the city worked to make the racers feel welcome. The scramble to house the thousands of competitors, officials and fans had started in early February. Chamber of Commerce Executive Director W. C. Schaeffer had announced that by the ninth of the month some 500 requests for reservations had been received, and asked residents for rooms to let at a rate of $5 to $10 per night.

Residents were hired to help the Sebring Firemen work the gates. Local realtor and insurance agent Harry Bailey published an item looking for those who would be willing to sell and take tickets, check cars, and perform the "duties connected with getting the huge crowds in and out of Hendricks Field" on Thursday, Friday, and Saturday. Workers would be paid, and could work one, two or all three days.

On the Thursday preceding the race, the Women's Club of Sebring held a dance at the municipal pier to provide entertainment for the Grand Prix visitors. The Highlandaires with Jimmy Eller furnished the music, and there was a floor show at intermission. Orange juice and Coca-Colas were available as refreshments. The ladies also set up food booths at Firemen's Field. It had been determined that race cars would be repaired there, instead of at the Air Terminal as in former years. On Friday evening, the senior class showed race films at the Sebring High School Auditorium for those interested in viewing the competition of previous years. Admission was 50-cents.

At the track, local Civil Defense Director Don Hansen made arrangements for a mobile C.D. Communications Unit with radio and telephone facilities. The nine-member hospital staff had the use of an American Red Cross mobile hospital unit from Miami, where "... even operations could be performed if necessary." It too was equipped with a radio, walkie talkie and telephone equipment. In a post race article, it was reportedly that "regrettably, the unit was used several times . . ."

Publicity was handled again by the Miami-based firm of Price and Cole (as it was in 1955). Julian Cole's wife, Diane Boulais—a 20-year-old professional model—was named the "Race Queen." The press had their facilities

Miss Sebring 1956, Diane Boulais proves that not all facets of road racing are hard work. Reprinted with permission of the Sebring Historical Society.

in a tent, and Western Union officials later reported that the combined press corps had sent out some 75,000 words. That, in addition to radio, television, and newsreel coverage.

Mrs. Venia Jean Serone, the niece of race chairman Allen C. Altvader, was scheduled for an appearance on the "Tonight Show," shown locally on WFLA-TV. She would invite then host Steve Allen and bandleader Skitch Henderson to attend the race.

Pre-race practice brought the usual number of problems to some of the entries. The Ferrari of Rubirosa and Pauley Mondial was slightly damaged in an encounter with a barrel marker while driven by a friend who was "trying out" the car.

One of the Morgans flipped during Thursday night practice; the driver was not seriously injured. Len Bastrup also flipped a brand-new Lotus Mark XI bouncing off a hay bale, then cartwheeling.

The Arnolt-Bristol team were "worried at length," when prior to leaving Chicago their cooling systems had not been drained adequately and as they passed through a blizzard that raged across the Northeast, the water froze, cracking the engine blocks on all four cars. That same storm blew across the Atlantic resulting in the elimination of the lone Alfa Romeo factory car. It was the first of the new cars sporting the 1300cc Guilietta Sprint engine and was aboard an Italian transport which ran aground in the bad weather.

One of the more impressive displays was put on by the Aston Martin team, who boasted English champions

Stirling Moss and Peter Collins as their pilots. They brought their own practical physicist. Pitmen said working with his slide rule, he could calculate within two laps when a tire would blow.

Highlands County's Bronze Saddle Club held a rodeo at the Air Terminal on race day. As the Firemen tried to snag football fans in the 1950 Sam Collier Memorial race, the local group had hopes of corralling race fans to watch the bucking broncs as well. Ads offered both the thrills of bull riding, horse riding and calf roping, plus ". . . a look at the fast-moving cars on track . . ."

Again, local hotels, motels, and private homes from Lake Placid to Lake Wales were bursting with the faithful. The *Highland County News* noted that some people had to take accommodations as far away as Lakeland and Haines City—but after coming thousands of miles to view or participate in the Grand Prix, driving extra miles would seem a "small inconvenience."

Reservation requests had been coming in as early as October,1955, and as race day approached, the chamber had been receiving as many as 50 letters a day looking for lodging. Officials predicted a 35% increase in the out-of-state crowd.

In fact, the Cubans reportedly were supposed to fly in their fans in ten planeloads, with another two Pan Am aircraft slated to come in from Puerto Rico. In the end, it was reported that the Air Terminal had a bumper day, with some 200 planes of various sizes flying in for the race.

It was another warm and sunny day as 27,000 people turned out to see a grueling race with what was at the time described as "the finest and most diverse field of sports cars and drivers ever assembled for a single race."

Famed American opera singer James Melton performed The Star-Spangled Banner, accompanied by the combined high school bands from Lake Placid and Sebring. He took a lap around the track in his vintage Stanley Steamer and served as the official race starter.

Strategic Air Command General Curtis LeMay had been asked to function as the official starter but was unable to serve. Apparently though, the general did find time to come in and view at least part of the race as a guest.

Fifty-eight of the fifty-nine starters roared off the line—all except for a Lotus driven by Joe Sheppard and William Smith. Apparently, their self-starter didn't work. They jacked up the car and turned the rear wheels to get the machine going—but were disqualified for making an unauthorized start.

First away was John Fitch in the souped-up "B" class Corvette with Englishman Mike Hawthorne in the D-Jaguar in hot pursuit. It wasn't long before the experienced Brit passed the American, and by the end of the first lap had secured the lead.

Around noon, Hawthorne made a lengthy pit stop, Moss moved to the point briefly but stopped for fuel and gave the wheel of the Aston Martin to co-driver Peter Collins, handing the lead to the 3.4 liter Ferrari of Fangio/Castelotti.

The yellow flag came out shortly after one o'clock when Carlos Menditeguy flipped his Maserati. Witnesses say it was a miracle he survived the crash. The Argentine was diagnosed with head injuries and a broken hand and was taken to the Weems Hospital in Sebring.

Minutes later, Peter Collins lost his mount when the gearbox seized in the Aston Martin. The car apparently had been run too hard, in an effort to push the leader.

Fangio stopped for gas on the 80th lap and gave the car over to Castellotti, allowing Desmond Titterington—who was driving with Hawthorne, to take the #8 Jaguar back out in front.

By 6 p.m., Fangio again had taken control of the Ferrari and the lead, and the battle between Ferrari and Jaguar continued into the night.

There were rumors of chaos again in the timing hut, but any problems in scoring were brought to a halt at 8 p.m., when Hawthorne brought the Jaguar into the pits with a broken fuel filter seal and non-existent brakes.

The Ferrari roared on into the night, and by the end of the race its brakes were spitting sparks. Reportedly, Castelotti pitted the car with just 45 minutes left and offered the wheel to Fangio. The world champ turned it down, telling his co-driver "Euginio, you finish. You've earned it." He then sat back, slapped a canvas hat on his balding head and lit a cigar. So, in the cool, breezy darkness, it was Castelotti who shot across the finish line for the victory.

The competition was run at a torrid pace, with an unprecedented rate of attrition, only 24 of the 60 original cars finished the 12-hour run. Ferrari had avenged their loss of a year before and were smart to hire the Argentine world champion. The car also broke the 1,000-mile mark for the first time in the once-around-the-clock competition.

The index of performance honors went to the #41 Porsche 550 Spyder driven by Hans Hermann and Wolfgang Von Trips—their car finished sixth overall, and first in their class.

Awards were handed out that year at the municipal pier. Ulmann, a linguist, introduced the winners in English, Italian, French, Spanish and German. The #17 Ferrari of Fangio and Castelotti took the lions' share of the

1956 Race Awards Ceremony—Castellotti (in dark glasses) and Fangio (both men in center of photo). Reprinted with permission of the Sebring Historical Society.

money—$3,000 for first place overall, and another $500 for finishing third in the handicap. Ferrari teammates Luigi Musso and Harry Schell finished second overall, that was good for another $1,500. The Hermann and Von Trips Porsche took $3,000 for winning the index of performance, while the #43 Porsche 550 Spyder of Jack McAfee and Pete Lovely won $1,500 for second in the handicap. Indy drivers Bob Sweikert and Jack Ensley won $500 for their third overall finish.

The American hope Corvette won the "B" division (they were the only entry), the production sports car category, and the team prize as well. Driver/Manager John Fitch later would comment that "It was less than we had hoped for but more than we deserved."

The end of the race did not finish the duties for champion Juan Fangio. Fellow Argentinian Carlos Menditeguy had sustained a double fracture of the head when his Maserati overturned in the esses during the race. Fangio stayed by his bedside at the Weems Hospital from Sunday until the following Tuesday, when Menditeguy's sister, Carla, and brother, Julio. arrived from Buenos Aires. The 41-year-old driver later was transferred to St. Mary's Hospital in West Palm Beach.

News accounts also chronicled an off-track death associated with the race; a 19-year-old was killed when the car he was riding in flipped over on State Road 98. Lyman Paul Duke and his companions had come to Sebring to see the grand prix.

Sportswriters contended that the race settled a number of popular arguments: First, it proved that America at last was capable of holding a true international event, worthy of being included in the international racing calendar; secondly, that the superlative performance of cars equipped with disc brakes must not be taken for granted on multi-cornered road circuits, and thirdly, American Indianapolis drivers apparently were able to become serious competitors in European style races—based on the third place performance by 1955 Indy winners Bob Sweikert and Jack Ensley.

Sweikert had come to Sebring to "see what this closed-course racing was all about." He noted that "Tough as it is, the brickyard does not have the car-killing problems of the airfield circuit—such as downshifting for curves." But Sweikert learned fast and used an Indianapolis trick which had the torsion bars of his Jaguar adjusted to allow him to skid through some of the turns without riding the brake pedal.

When it was all over, he had good words for both the race and its competitors:

"I liked it at Sebring. Those drivers are all gentlemen. If you came up behind a slower car . . . they let you go by and give you a wave. Up here, we're courteous and we're gentlemen but moving out of the groove? We don't do that."

Sweikert had learned a lot from Fangio and offered him a chance to drive at Indianapolis in one of his two entries. Fangio said he would have liked to do it but had other commitments on that date. Ironically, the Indy champ died just three months later, killed in a sprint car mishap in Salem, Indiana, when his car jumped a guardrail.

In June 1956, a contingent of Sebring residents went to Indianapolis to talk with officials of the 500, to see if there were ways to make the 12 Hour competition run more smoothly. Among them were Allen Altvader, Ford Heacock, Frank Bryant, and Sheriff Broward Coker.

Another kind of racing was held in a special event in July, as the Bronze Saddle Club—known throughout the region for their rodeos—held a horse race at the arena grounds of the Sebring Air Terminal.

1957

In 1957, the 12 Hours of Sebring really had begun to come into its own. Then Florida Governor LeRoy Collins declared March 18-23 as Florida International Sports Car Race Week, to be climaxed with the Florida International 12 Hour Grand Prix of Endurance for Amoco.

The sports car world was abuzz that former teammates Juan Fangio and Eugenio Castelotti would not be in the same car but instead would duke it out on the track at Sebring in separate vehicles. Castelotti was still with Ferrari, but Fangio had moved over to the Maserati squad.

The Ferrari team again had gotten the jump on the competition by winning the first FIA Manufacturer's Endurance Cup race of the year in Buenos Aires, Fangio's native Argentina. However, hopes of Sebring's potential duel were dashed just prior to the mid-March competition, when word came that Castelotti had been killed while testing his new machine in Modena, Italy. Reportedly, the driving ace missed a curve and slammed into a concrete wall.

There was additional bad news when it was learned that the English Aston Martin team had withdrawn two cars because they could not meet the new specifications in time for the race.

But none of this seemed to dampen the enthusiasm of the fans or sponsors. The *Highlands County News* reported that new bleachers were being built, fences were being strung, there were telephone and power lines brought in and re-routed, and American Oil, the sponsor for the second year in a row and the official fuel for the race, was installing gas pumps and digging holes for the placement of underground fuel tanks.

The Mobile Home Manufacturing Association had donated a fleet of trailers that were being used for everything from press facilities such as mobile radio studios and wirephoto outlets to VIP suites. General Motors used three of them.

The Sebring Hospitality Committee reported that even with residents offering to rent spare rooms, there still were more requests than lodgings.

Race Chairman Frank Bryant announced that his group had come up with a way to deal with those who came for Thursday and Friday time trials, then did not leave. On Thursday, tickets would be sold in groups of three, on Friday, groups of two. Those who did not wish to come on the remaining days would be able to redeem those passes at the gate which would stay open 24-hours, beginning on Thursday morning.

Although there was still general admission parking, the notion of reserved parking was introduced that year, with Ford Heacock taking care of advanced sale tickets from his office on the circle, downtown.

The Sebring High School Seniors again showed movies of the races. They included the 1954, 1955, and 1956 Grand Prix, along with films of *Le Mans* and other sports car races. The presentation again was in the school's auditorium, the price was 25-cents, and programs also were available at the door.

Even the merchants got involved, closing at noon on Saturday for employees who wanted to go to the races. Stores stayed open Wednesday afternoon and late Friday night as well to help make up for the missed hours. The Hotel Sebring coffee shop was open 24 hours a day, and the Highlands County News was packed with merchants' ads welcoming race fans and offering race week specials.

A parade had been planned for the downtown area, but the processional was called off by Mayor J.D. Hunt and Community Committee Chairman Don Hansen due to the crush of traffic created by grand prix fans arriving for the race.

There was more prize money offered that year as well—$3,000 each for the overall winners and the index of performance winners, plus the overall winners would be presented with the silver Amoco trophy—valued at $5,000. The prize for second place in overall and index of performance was set at $1,500, with $500 allocated to third place in each category.

Firestone Tire & Rubber Company offered $1,000 each to the overall and index of performance winners, provided the cars were using Firestone tires.

There were notables both on and off the track. Famous bandleader Paul Whitman was in town, along with ranking FIA members Count Johnnie Lorani of Milan, Italy, and Harold Parker from London's Royal Automobile Club. It was noted that Whitman spent three days at Lake Brentwood Court while in Highlands County to see the races. Owners noted that Whiteman had "chosen one of the finest motor courts in the state in the finest little town." Well known

Race publicist Reggie Smith is at the wheel, taking some officials around the paddock during the 1957 Race. The car had been designated for the Clerk of the Course. Note the Amoco sticker on the windshield. (Bill Foster Collection)

CBS radio and telecaster Walter Cronkite was scheduled to do four 15-minute broadcasts during the race, while Bill Sweet would handle the microphone for NBC's Monitor radio show. They would be joined by radio reports around the world on the Voice of America, plus journalists from Associated Press, United Press International, Reuters, and the Australian Associated press.

There were press parties galore. Friday at Kenilworth Lodge there was a fête hosted by the Rolls Royce Company. That night at the Elks Club there was another function. Walter Cronkite was among the notables who

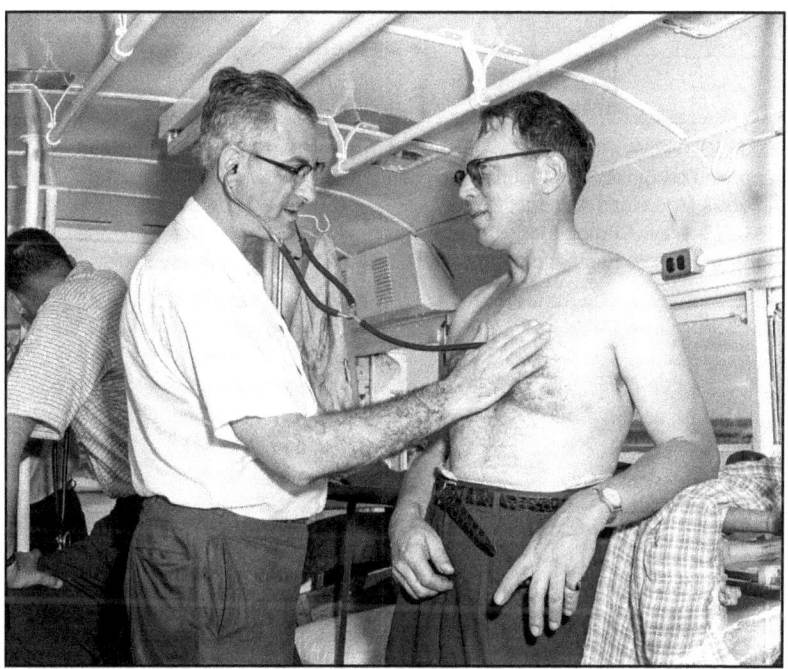

Even in 1957, drivers were mandated to get a pre-race physical, to make certain they were in good enough shape to withstand their turn on the bumpy five-mile circuit that was Sebring. (Bill Foster Collection)

TELLING THE WORLD—Ace commentators **Art Peck** and **Walter Conkrite** (above) report the progress of the Sebring race on the C.B.S. network with assist from Amoco's Moore and Aldridge. (Rubin)
IT GOES—says **Stirling Moss** (right) to designer **Zora Duntov** after trying the special Corvette in 1957. Reprinted with permission of the Sebring Historical Society.

Everybody seemed to sense that Sebring had the makings of the great racing event it has become today. Here is Alec Ulmann, father of the race with Mary Hulman, daughter of Tony Hulman, owner of the Indianapolis track and Harry Hartz, one of the all-time greats of the Indianapolis Speedway and other major racing circuits. Reprinted with permission of the Sebring Historical Society.

watched Texas Driver Carroll Shelby receive a silver tray from representatives of *Sports Illustrated* magazine for "advancement among world sports car drivers."

George Schrafft was there, although he was better known for his forays in the restaurant and candy business than for his driving prowess. John Weitz, the New York fashion designer, also was at Sebring to compete in the event. The young, 21-year-old Lance Reventlow, the son of millionairess Barbra Hutton, was allowed to drive. He previously had been blacklisted by the SCCA the year before for "misrepresenting his age." However, the FIA had cabled Ulmann to issue him a license for the competition.

This year there was to be an all-woman team as Mlle. Gilbert Thirion, Belgium's champion woman driver, entered her Renault Dauphin. Thirion had won her division the year before at Italy's famous *Mille Miglia*. She would be joined at the wheel by Nadge Ferrier of Switzerland.

Interestingly enough, the former Monte Carlo winner, Greta Molander, had stopped in Sebring on her way to France a year before, surveying the course with an eye toward fielding an all-woman team for a 12-hour event.

Apparently, she never returned.

The first woman ever to compete at Sebring was back, Isabelle Haskell—who in order to drive, had listed herself formerly from England & West Palm Beach, now she claimed her original residence— Red Barn, New Jersey. She also had a new husband—none other than the famous Italian driver Alejandro de Thomaso. They had shared the wheel of a Maserati 150S the year before, but the car completed only 15 laps before retiring with transmission problems.

Another woman also was scheduled to take her turn at the 1957 12 Hours, Denise McCluggage, a writer for the *New York Herald Tribune* would sign-on, but would not actually get on track until the following year. As always, Sebring's share of nobility had returned, including Germany's Baron Fritz Huschke von Hanstein and Count Wolfgang Von Tripps, the Marquis Alfonse de Portago of Spain, and Sir Sidney and Lady Greta Oakes from Bermuda.

One competitor who was conspicuous by his absence was playboy and former competitor, Porfirio Rubirosa, who withdrew shortly before the race.

Locals look on as the 1957 Ferrari team unloads one of their 315S models at the Stiles-Jonson Ponitac dealership on South Ridgewood Drive in the downtown Sebring area where they were paddocked that year. (Bill Foster Collection)

Practices were held for two days, with a great deal of interest paid to the principal car makers—Maserati, Jaguar, and Ferrari. It was the defending champ, Fangio, who turned the quickest lap at 3:25.8 in his new 4.5 litre Maserati. Mike Hawthorne made the best lap for Jaguar at 3:29.4. By race day, some of the greatest drivers of 14 nations were listed plus the United States, driving some 20 makes of cars, manufactured in five countries.

Spectators had more to look at during the race, as promoters staged an "International Automobile Exposition," with 75 to 100 makes and models of cars on display at the Air Terminal. According to newspaper reports, Ford Heacock estimated that 25,000 people turned out for the 7th annual running of the Florida Grand Prix, although later estimates range as high as 35,000. It was a hot and sunny day as the countdown began for the mad dash of drivers to cars in the *Le Mans* start.

The pit crew can make or break a driver. An interesting angle to watch is how these boys replenish gas, oil, and water, change a complete set of wheels, clean the windshield and make other adjustments in a matter of seconds. Reprinted with permission of the Sebring Historical Society.

Peter Collins roared away from the thundering pack in his Ferrari 315, while Englishman Mike Hawthorne was the last car off the line, his Jaguar refusing to start. By the end of the first lap, Collins' Ferrari had built a 15-second lead over Moss in the Maserati. Jean Behra's Maserati Monza overtook Collins just past the one-hour mark to head the early competition, building an initial lead of about ten seconds. He dominated for the next three hours, turning the car over to Fangio at about 2:00 with a 2-lap lead that they would never relinquish.

During the race, several photographers were standing at the Hairpin to get some closeup of the cars at slower speeds. The guys had a cooler with some Coca-Colas in it. As they were drinking some Cokes, Stirling Moss came by and gave them the "I'd like a drink" symbol by putting his hand to his mouth. One of the photographers, the world-famous Bernard Cahier, had an idea. On the next lap, Cahier had opened a Coke and as Moss came by at the Hairpin, Cahier handed him the soda! Moss promptly drank the Coke and when he came back around, he tossed it out at the Hairpin in the grass so the guys could retrieve it. As Moss headed down to Webster Turn, he gave them a wave as thanks! Luckily, one of the photographers thought to take a picture of the incident for posterity! Reprinted with permission of the Sebring Historical Society.

At exactly 10 p.m., under a brilliant display of fireworks, it was four-time world champion, Juan Fangio, repeating his winning performance in 1956, this time with co-driver Jean Behra. Ferrari, who had won with Fangio at the wheel the year before, managed no better than fourth. In the winner's circle, Behra literally fell into Fangio's arms and the two champions could not stop congratulating each other amidst the bursts of the photographers' flashbulbs.

It would be the first and only win ever for the Maserati marque at the 12 Hours of Endurance. Behra had set a sizzling pace, flying around the 5.2-mile airport circuit, and breaking the course record twice in the early going. On laps 20 and 27 he turned identical times of 3:24:30 for an average speed of 92 mph. In all, the team covered 197 laps, for more than 1024 miles, at an average speed of 85.4 mph.

Taking the index of performance cash and trophy were Americans Art Bunker and Charlie Wallace in a Porsche RS. The duo finished eighth overall.

Trophies were handed out Sunday morning at "a dinner" on Sebring's municipal pier. Of course, Alec Ulmann was the master of ceremonies.

It was in 1957 that the race recorded the first on-track track fatality. 33-year-old Bob Goldich lost control of his Arnolt-Bristol in the esses. The car hit the sand barrier, then flipped twice. Goldich, a father of two, was pronounced dead on arrival at the Weems Hospital in Sebring. The rest of the Arnolt team immediately withdrew.

Post race nuptials also were reported. Roy Jackson-Moore, 31, of Glendale, California (formerly Liverpool,

England) was married to Denise Netherwood of Yorkshire, England. County Judge Mervin Rehrer performed the ceremony on Monday following the race.

Compliments were handed out all around at the close of the 1957 event. Officials of the Chamber of Commerce praised the local merchants and hoteliers for not gouging the crowd. Several letters from participants and spectators on the same subject were later published in the *Highlands County News*. The Sebring Firemen received a very complimentary letter from Melbourne Martin of the American Title & Insurance Corporation, who pointed out how smoothly the whole event was run. A letter to the editor of the *Highlands County News* by Business & Professional Women's Club representative Carol Beck complimented the Sebring Police Department for their hard work as well.

But the racing was not over at Sebring. There had been several other smaller road races at various times on the air terminal's circuit, such as the Miami Sports Car Club's 25-lap event in January dubbed "Little Sebring."

But in May 1957, another kind of racing made its debut on the historic track. The Highlands Rod Benders, Inc. held their first drag race at the track. The group actually was formed on March 29, 1957. Some of the officers included President Frank Ferrell, Vice President William H. Frazier, Traffic Manager Bill Sircy, and Publicity Director Jim Logan.

The gates opened at noon on May 12, with time trials at 12:30 and eliminations starting at 3:00. There was a little something for everybody, with 20 different classes listed.

Also in May, the course received a little help as Highlands County Commissioners voted to pave a portion of the circuit—providing there would be another grand prix sports car race there in 1958.

In June, another similar group out of Miami held a similar event as the South Florida Timing Association conducted a meet at Sebring. Hometown boy Bill Sircy won in the "competition coupe" division.

The Sebring Lions Club had a chance to look at different views on the races in July. They first watched an Amoco movie of the 1957 endurance classic, then later watched a So-Cal Productions film, shot by car on the streets and alleys of the city itself.

On July 25, Ford Heacock announced that the race date for 1958 would be March 22. Sebring's Pink McAdams was dubbed the Race Chairman for that event.

PRIX OF ENDURANCE FOR THE AMOCO TROPHY

Timetable of Events, 1958

Saturday, February 15	Midnight	Entries Close
Monday, March 17	10:00 A.M. to 6:00 P.M.	*Registration* at Race Headquarters
Tuesday, March 18	10:00 A.M. to 6:00 P.M. 10:00 A.M. to 5:00 P.M.	*Registration* at Race Headquarters *Medical and Technical Inspections*
Wednesday, March 19	10:00 A.M. to 6:00 P.M. 10:00 A.M. to 5:00 P.M. 1:30 P.M. to 4:00 P.M.	*Registration* at Race Headquarters *Medical and Technical Inspections* *Daytime Practice*
Thursday, March 20	10:00 A.M. to 6:00 P.M. 1:30 P.M. to 4:00 P.M. 7:00 P.M. to 9:00 P.M. 9:30 P.M.	*Registration* at Race Headquarters *Daytime Practice* *Night Practice* *Grand Prix Ball* at Pier Auditorium
Friday, March 21	10:00 A.M. 1:00 P.M. No Official Practice	Historical Automobile Cavalcade Concours d'Elegance Historical Automobile Driving Tests Day reserved for final course preparation
Saturday, March 22	7:30 A.M. 9:30 A.M. **10:00 A.M.** 6:30 P.M. 10:00 P.M.	*Race cars assemble at pits* *Drivers' briefing. Flag-raising ceremony.* **Race begins** *Car lights to be turned on* *Race finishes*
Sunday, March 23	12:00 M. 1:00 P.M.	*Posting of results* at Pier Auditorium *Distribution of awards* at Pier Auditorium

This race counts in points for the F.I.A. WORLD SPORTS CAR MANUFACTURERS' CHAMPIONSHIP

Other races so designated in 1958:

1,000 km.	Buenos Aires, Argentina	January 26
Mille Miglia	Italy	May 11
1,000 km.	Nurburgring, Germany	June 1
24 Hours	Le Mans, France	June 15
Swedish Grand Prix	Sweden	August 10
Tourist Trophy Race	Great Britain	September 13
Venezuelan Grand Prix	Venezuela	November 9

1958

It had been said that Sebring embraced the race, but by 1958 it had become virtually a status symbol. Local residents were given first crack at tickets and parking spaces, as the race sales office opened in the mezzanine of the Sebring Hotel on Tuesday and Wednesday, January 14 and 15 of that year, so that citizens could pick up bleacher reservations and parking passes.

Applications already had been coming in by mail, with officials starting to fulfill those requests the following Thursday.

The *Highlands County News* reported that the Sebring Chamber of Commerce also was looking to update their accommodations lists from private homes and other sources, to handle the thousands of fans who were expected in for the 7th annual running of the Florida Grand Prix of Endurance.

It was in mid-February that the Grand Prix headquarters opened at the municipal pier. Alec Ulmann and his wife Mary had arrived to address the details of the year's most important road racing competition.

To start things off, Ulmann had secured permission from the Sebring City Council to build four permanent observation towers at key sites around the 5.2-mile circuit. This was to facilitate better public address, newspaper, photo, and radio coverage of the event. The construction was underwritten by the Triumph Motor Company. By the time Race Week arrived, the town had "put on the dog." The Sebring Garden Club again had decorated both the race and press headquarters, and held a "Strolling Flower Show," with different arrangements in the windows of downtown stores. A week-full of events was planned as well, from Monday's registration to Saturday's running of the once-around-the-clock classic. Two new events were added in 1958, a Grand Prix Ball and an Historic Auto Cavalcade complete with "*concours d'elegance*—a parade of expertly restored and unusual automobiles"—coupled with a veteran car driving test.

The Grand Prix Ball was dubbed "The Social Event of Race Week." It was staged by the Junior Women's Club of Sebring, working with Mary Ulmann. It was to be held at the municipal pier auditorium from 9:30 Thursday night until 1:30 Friday morning. Dance music was provided by Jimmy Thompson and his orchestra, with a 'floor show' included. Mrs. Ford Heacock performed a "vocal specialty," Virginia Foster Hendrick did a dance number entitled Blues

& Boogie, and Mrs. Edna Clarke did an impersonation of Sophie Tucker.

The highlight of the evening was the crowning of Miss Sebring Grand Prix, Betty Frazee of Silver Springs. She had been selected during "The Great Triangle Rally" by the Sports Car Club of America earlier that month. Frazee performed as a mermaid at the popular Silver Springs tourist attraction and had appeared on such network television programs such as *Today* with Dave Garroway, *Tonight* on CBS, NBC's *Arlene Francis Show,* and had done some underwater scenes on the TV series *Sea Hunt.*

Among the 400 in attendance at the Ball were broadcaster Walter Cronkite, along with drivers Stirling Moss, Jean Behra, Porfirio Rubirosa, Count Wolfgang von Tripps, and Carol Shelby—they and others were introduced to the crowd by Ulmann.

There was one sour note. It was reported that during a race party hosted by the Sebring Chamber of Commerce, most of the 15 pastel caricatures of famous race drivers done by the famous artist Zito of Palm Beach had been stolen off the walls.

The Auto Cavalcade was scheduled for Friday, featuring cars dating back more than half a century. The centerpiece was to be a 1903 Stanley Steamer, with a number of other vehicles of various vintage and other interesting machines. Prizes were to be handed out to the oldest cars, the cars that came from the greatest distance, and winners of several driving events.

The competitions were overseen by Smith Hempstone Oliver—former Automobile Section Curator at the Smithsonian Museum of Washington DC, and an alumni of other Sebring races in various capacities. Among the tests of car and driver were "the reverse wiggle-woggle," wherein the cars would weave in and out around a series of pylons, reversing directions twice. There also was a four-fold parking test, a zig-zag course running test, touch & go, acceleration & braking, a quarter-mile sprint and a slow speed in high gear event. Following the exhibition, the cars were to be placed on display for fans in the raceway's paddock area.

The Paddock had been upgraded for the 1958 affair. There was a special parking area, seating, and dining facilities. The price also had been upgraded—it cost $10 to get in.

But the paddock was not the only improvement at the track that year. A new three-deck officials tower had been built on the front straightaway. It would carry the sponsorship of Jaguar as part of a 15-year contract.

The Automobile Racing Club of Florida
announces the opening of
Les Douze Heures
a bistro located in the Paddock, serving delicious dinners from noon until about 8:30 P.M.
Relax and enjoy yourselves for the modest sum of $3.50.
The menu is:

Coupe Tomae
Prime Ribs of Western Beef au Jus
Haricots Verts
Pommes Neufs
or
Home Baked Ham with Sweet Potatoes
Salade Saison
Pecan Pie   Apple Pie
Ice Cream
Coffee

Those who wanted international cuisine could have a taste in the Sebring paddock. Reprinted with permission of the Sebring Historical Society.

There were two new bridges, and four new grandstands added around the circuit. The main straightaway bleachers were enlarged, and stands were put up in the tower turn, at the esses, near the hairpin and at the famous Webster corner.

A pedestrian overpass was built near the esses. MG provided the sponsorship on that one, it bore the slogan "Safety Fast." A new vehicular overpass across the front straightaway near the pit area also had been added. That came at an estimated cost of $10,000 and was put up by the Martini & Rossi Italian vermouth manufacturer.

In 1958, Coca-Cola sponsored the scoreboard in an effort to keep teams, the media, fans, and others on the most up to date standings during the 12-hour grind. (Bill Foster Collection)

Special reserved front row parking was set aside in eight areas along the main straightaway and in other sections of the course.

There were many new features and ideas incorporated in the race as organizers became more sophisticated. The first year that Pass Out tickets were used at the front gate for those leaving and returning to the track was 1958.

The local community participated in concessions at the track. The Sebring American Legion had a booth open there all race week, as did the Lions Club, and even the Sebring Women's Club—they offered "home-cooked pies and other delectables."

Waco Import Cars of Miami also set up a "hospitality area" for the general public. It was one of the first ever recorded at the track. Fans were invited to come and relax in the shade of their "Exhibition Tent." Naturally, there were autos on display, and salespeople were available to answer any questions fans might have about the cars.

The *Highlands County News* also expanded their coverage, producing a special race edition of the paper. It was a "B" section designed for local residents, race fans, and for mail-outs around the world. It contained line-ups, race schedules, and many feature articles. One piece noted that the number 13 had never been assigned at the Sebring Grand Prix and indicating exactly how the car numbers were allocated. Another outlined provisions for insurance coverage for racers, teams, and officials at the track.

Again, this year, many of the functions would be housed in trailers provided by the Mobile Home Manufacturer's Association, including units for VIP's, first aid, and the media. The Civil Defense and Red Cross teamed up to provide two medical locations—one for the racers, the other for spectators.

This also was the first year that the local radio station would be recognized as an integral part of the event. Ulmann, John Reeves, the president of the Mobile Home Manufacturer's Association, and Al Frank, the manager of local station WJCM combined to announce the formation of the cooperative Sebring International Sports car Radio Network.

Reeves, a former radio personality himself, would head the broadcast which was done on and around the four new observation towers built by the Triumph Motor Company prior to the race.

The big debate over the 1958 12 Hours, was whether back-to-back winner and defending champion Juan Fangio would compete in the seventh annual running. In February, the *Highlands County News* published an article that indicated he would be there if he could find a suitable car to drive.

The world champion later was kidnapped by Cuban rebels and held captive so that he could not compete at a race in Havanna. That February 24 competition was cut short when a driver went off course into a group of spectators, killing a number of them. Fangio was released a short time after the race was halted.

It was rumored in the Argentine press that Fangio had been considering retirement from active competition and would forsake both Sebring and the Indianapolis 500. That speculation turned all eyes to Fangio's former teammate,

Frenchman Jean Behra. He'd shared the winning seat with Fangio in a Maserati the year before, breaking the track's single-lap speed record twice. This year he was scheduled to drive a much smaller Porsche RS with Edgar Barth.

Finally, a week before the race, the word came that Fangio would not be there to contend for the Amoco Trophy in 1958.

But he was not the only long-time competitor that would not make it to the race. Among the "old-timers that would be missed," as the newspapers put it, was Spanish nobleman Marquis Alfonso de Portago, who was killed at the famous *Mille Miglia* shortly after the 1957 running of the 12 Hours, and Piero Taruffi "The Silver Fox" who had retired from competition after winning that same race. Reporters noted he would be best remembered for pushing his Lancia across the finish line in the 1954 race, only to be disqualified.

But for the famous drivers who were not there, an impressive line-up of competitors had signed on for the endurance classic. Included were Englishman and former winner Stirling Moss, the German Baron Fritz Huschke von Hanstein, Alexander de Tomaso, Roy Salvadori, Belgian Oliver Gendebein, and Americans and former winners Briggs Cunningham and Carol Shelby to name a few.

In all, 16-countries were to be represented in one way or another in this truly international event. There were 65 cars set for the starting grid, among them there were 27 English, 25 Italian, seven German, four American, and two French vehicles.

There were nearly 46,000 fans on hand by the time race day arrived. Famous broadcasters on hand to cover the event included veteran reporter Walter Cronkite, and *Today Show host*, Dave Garroway.

Many cars came by ocean freighters. They were unloaded in Miami and driven to Sebring for the race. Reprinted with permission of the Sebring Historical Society.

The contingent of law enforcement officers continued to grow in an effort to manage the ever-increasing throng of fans and dignitaries. Highlands County Sheriff Broward Coker had arranged for 125 additional law enforcement officers. There was a 64-man unit from the Miami Auxiliary, sheriff's deputies from Hillsborough and Hardee Counties, a group of motorcycle police officers from Marion County, plus municipal police from neighboring Polk County, with others coming from as far away as Brooksville.

Extra Fire units also had been provided, with engines from the City of Sebring, the Avon Park Bombing Range, and the US Division of Forestry.

The safety units were connected with the use of walkie talkies operating from a pair of different base stations.

The opening ceremonies included music from the Sebring High School Band, and a performance of the Star-Spangled Banner by opera star James Melton. Florida Governor LeRoy Collins was made the official starter and dropped the green flag.

At the *Le Mans* start, it was the #14 Ferrari 250TR of Peter Collins and Phil Hill that was first away. But he soon was caught and passed by fellow Englishman Stirling Moss who then blistered the circuit not once, but twice for a new single lap record. He turned the 5.2-mile course in 3:20 flat for a speed of 93.6mph.

The Stirling Moss/Tony Brooks Aston Martin DBR1 led for the first four hours, but finally retired with gearbox troubles, handing the lead back to the #14 Ferrari of the Collins/Hill team, who cruised to victory. It was their second win in as many races for the coveted manufacturer's title, taking the opening race of the season at Buenos Aires in January. They also set a new course record, covering 200 laps for 1,040 miles at an average speed of 88.67mph.

There was only one serious accident that year. Chet Flynn locked the brakes on his #23 Ferrari. The General Motors executive rolled off course, suffering head, shoulder, and a bad eye injury.

At the awards ceremony held on the municipal pier, Peter Collins and Phil Hill not only took the $3,000 for the overall win, plus the Amoco Trophy, they also received a Firestone Trophy for their efforts.

Picking up the KLG Index of Performance trophy and another $3,000 check was Alejandro & Isabell de Tomaso of West Palm Beach. They had driven the OSCA 750S with the help of Robert Ferguson of Columbus, Ohio. Isabell's maiden name was Haskell, and she had been the first female driver at the Sebring races. With this victory she now became the first member of the distaff side to share in the silverware of the event.

Firestone gave them a trophy, and also a trophy to the winners of the Grand Touring Division—the Paul O'Shea/Bruce Kessler/Dave Cunningham Ferrari. The Nisonger Trophy went to the 3-car Austin Healy GT effort, for the highest aggregate number of laps by a complete, official, three-car team. One of those vehicles had a longtime racer and original Sebring race organizer, Phil Stiles, as a driver.

Despite kudos the previous year that local restaurants, hotels, and other retail outlets had not upped their prices during race week, inspectors from the state's Hotel & Restaurant Commission were in town to police pricing practices. A *Highlands County News* article indicated that the Sebring Chamber of Commerce had made the request—citing several complaints from 1957, and saying that they wanted to avoid any recurrence of the problem.

The *'News'* also noted that three recently married couples would be spending their honeymoons at the races. Canadian Ross de St Croix, the President of the Montreal MG Car Club brought his new wife, Andrew Ewing jr. of Nashville, Tennessee, and his bride would be there, and the new Mr. & Mrs. Robert W. Leary. He was a photographer for *Christophorus* magazine—the European Porsche publication. A special article was planned (with photographs, of course) to be printed later.

Again in 1958, the end of the '12 Hours' did not signal the end of racing at the track. A seven-state regional drag racing meet was booked in for mid-June. Unfortunately, most of the events were washed out by the summer rains, and the balance of the competition was moved to Miami.

The *Highlands County News* did note that the drag racers had enough time to name their own beauty contest winner—Joyce Kuhman—an attractive Boynton Beach brunette.

In October of 1958, Goodyear Tire and Rubber Company asked to use the track for testing.

Longtime Race Secretary Reggie Smith came to the Sebring City Council to obtain permission. It would be the first time the circuit had been rented by a corporation for private use. A committee of Smith, Air Terminal Manager Alan Altvader, and Airport Supervisory Committeeman David Starrett were appointed to make provisions.

They decided that:
1) Goodyear would pay a $100 per hour fee, with the Air Terminal to provide flagmen and to clean the course.
2) There would be a minimum charge of $50 if the test was called off, and a minimum overall charge of $1,000 for the test program.
3) Goodyear was to give a 7-day notice of their intentions so that the course might be put in shape and arrangements be made to allow for the least amount of inconvenience to the permanent Air Terminal tenants.
4) That Goodyear provides liability insurance.

It was never indicated whether or not the company took the city up on their offer.

The year 1958 also was the first occurrence of talk that there might be a second Sebring race. Alec Ulmann made the announcement at the beginning of race week. The plan was to have a world cup drivers' championship race in 1959, the day following the annual 12-hour competition for sports cars. The Indianapolis 500 was one of the competitions designated for points in this series.

This was to be a race for Formula One and Formula Two Grand Prix cars, single-seat vehicles using aviation fuel. They were quite different from the two-seater sport models designed for regular roads that ran the endurance race.

It would be known as the Grand Prix of the United States.

In the fall, word came that the period for the grand prix-style drivers' cup race would be moved back to the end of 1959. The reasons given were that it would be difficult to get the cars prepared in time for March, and that accommodation during race week was already scarce enough, and the re-scheduling of the competition would ease the housing problem.

Even while all this was going on, track improvements continued to be made. New concrete box seats were constructed above the pit areas, a new emergency hospital facility was being built, and a permanent-press box was to be installed.

The eyes of Sebring and the world were focused on 1959.

As the race developed over the years, there were ongoing efforts to turn the makeshift circuit into a for purpose racecourse. In 1958, Highlands County donated some of their road maintenance equipment to widen and improve parts of the twisting and challenging raceway. (Bill Foster Collection)

1959

The format for the 1959 race activities was set to follow the activities of the year before. In addition to the regular practice times, tech and medical inspections, there would be another Grand Prix Ball and a second Historic Auto Cavalcade. A *Highlands County News* article noted that many imported car displays had been planned (probably after seeing the success of the WACO tent in 1958), and there were additions being made for fans in the paddock, as that area continued to be upgraded.

For instance, there was the establishment of the Paddock Club. It provided an 'extra' for the fans wanting special concession services, food, and beverages in a race headquarters atmosphere. There also were to be pit box seats, built three-tiers high atop the pits. These would provide an excellent view of the spectacular *Le Mans* start.

Paddock bleachers were also being built for fans to view the races.

There were a few sour notes in the early months. The Sebring City Council, The Airport Advisory Committee, and the Sebring Firemen Inc, got together for a joint meeting in January. At first, the subject was to be the Firemen's sub-lease of the racetrack to the Automobile Racing Club of Florida. However, it had been rumored that the council might not have been 100% behind the race. Reports after the meeting indicated that the men had an amicable session, and all agreed that the grand prix was an asset to the community.

The council also again gave the go ahead to have Race Headquarters at the Sebring pier. Apparently, there had been some talk about putting it at the fairgrounds—a suggestion that caused race secretary Reginald Smith to balk. Council's OK of the pier pleased Smith, who referred to it as "Sebring's front door" and noting the favorable impression it would make on race visitors from around the globe. By the end of January, it had been reported that motels in and around the city had already been booked solidly.

As in 1958, Don O'Reilly was the Director of Press Relations. He announced that Southern Bell would install a teletype at the track for use by the press corps. Press facilities were provided by the Mobile Home Manufacturing Association, it was dubbed the "solid gold trailer." The mobile press unit was valued at a whopping $50,000. Highlands County Sheriff Broward Coker was called in to assure its safe delivery to the track. Reports indicated that as many as 800 correspondents, reporters, and photographers were expected in from all points of the globe to record the 12 Hours of Sebring race.

There were 89 stations across the country that would carry the nation's oldest European-style road race. They were featured on the CBS network, with the venerated Walter Cronkite to do their announcing. The famous newsman also would be a racing competitor, taking a stint behind the wheel of a Lancia Appia-Zagato with co-drivers Peter Baumberger and Warren Rohlfs. New York sportsman and auto dealer Charlie Kreisler had entered the car.

Receiving the crown as the queen of the 1959 Grand Prix was Sue Bowden of Cypress Gardens. Originally from Shaw, Mississippi, she would receive the tiara from retiring queen Betty Frazee. Frazee, who had been featured at another Florida tourist attraction—Silver Springs—had her sights set on another title. She was in the running for Miss Florida Citrus that year.

The Second Historic Cavalcade would also be held that year, this time under the auspices of Col. Tim Hawkins. He announced that 90 of the oldest cars in the world would be featured at the event. An 1893 Benz Velo would be displayed as the oldest vehicle. Several vintage racers also were scheduled to be there, including the winner of the 1914 Lyons Grand Prix—a car owned by Briggs Cunningham.

There also would be the mandatory round of parties. Just as in 1958, a press party was held at the Sebring VFW clubhouse. As entertainment, a representative of *Time* was to show slides from the magazine's files. A chronograph was given as a door prize, it was won by *Sports Car Illustrated* writer John Christy. Christy also drove an Austin Healy Sprite in the GT4 division.

Frank Fassett's Trio provided music.

The guests were suitably impressed by the affair. They were quoted in the *Highlands County News* as calling it "the best of the annual parties" . . . The Junior Women's Club, with the able help of Mary Ulmann, who was to oversee the arrangements. Music was to be provided by The Sandpipers of Lakeland, with door prizes also to be given away.

In conjunction with the races, Ed Boyd, the manager of the Florida Theatre, announced there would be a special showing of the production *Men With Cars*, a film of the 1958 12 Hours of Sebring as chronicled by five different cameramen.

MARY ULMANN—financial adviser to the Sebring project. "Without her we would never have made it," says husband Alec. Reprinted with permission of the Sebring Historical Society.

As race week drew closer, there was such an influx of visitors that Sebring's mayor, J.D. Hunt, appealed to residents to leave their cars at home except in emergencies, to provide additional parking spaces "for the sports car clan." The newspaper also noted that the normal Florida weather had "been missing in recent days," a euphemism for the downpour that had inundated the area for most of the week, but writers predicted better conditions in time for the '12 Hours.' Sebring wasn't the only place that had severe weather. At least two teams, the three-car Lotus factory effort, and the entry of Alejandro de Tomaso were late not arriving until Friday, their ships had battled raging Atlantic storms.

One former competitor who would watch from the sidelines was René Bonnet. He had been the first international contender at the '12 Hours,' but in 1959 came to Sebring on crutches. Bonnet was recovering from serious injuries he suffered in a September 1958 truck accident. Bonnet's Deutsch-Bonnet cars captured the Index of Performance trophies in the 1952 inaugural event, and then again, the following year.

Although there was no qualifying, it was noted that Stirling Moss and Lance Reventlow took little notice of the track during Wednesday practice, tying for the best practice time at 3:52 for the 5.2-mile course—an average speed of better than 80 miles per hour. Moss piloted a new Lister-Jag, while Reventlow drove a Ferrari 250 Testa Rosa.

René Dreyfus, a former French racing champion and Indianapolis competitor was the honorary starter for the event.

The hopes of the newswriters were not realized, and it was a cloudy day with heavy rain. Apparently, that dampened the enthusiasm of the fans only slightly as more than 40,000 people showed up to watch America's premier sports car competition.

A light fog settled in at the track, as the maximum allowable 65 cars lined up on the front straightaway for the traditional *Le Mans* start. Again, the Sebring High School Band provided musical entertainment for the opening ceremonies, with opera star James Melton again recruited to sing the Star-Spangled Banner.

When the green flag dropped, the Aston Martin DBR1 of Englishman Roy Salvadori and Carroll Shelby of Texas took the early lead, relinquishing after just four laps to the Ferrari 250 TR of former winner Jean Behra and his co-driver Cliff Allison. They held the point for ten laps but were overtaken by another of the Ferrari team—the Phil Hill/Oliver Gendebien entry when Behra ended up in a six-minute pit stop. Word was that the Testa Rosa's starter switch balked.

The two Ferraris diced for the front with the powerful Lister-Jag of Stirling Moss and Ivor Bueb. Phil Hill's entry gave up the ghost shortly after he turned his fastest circuit of the day when the car's axel broke about 2:30 in the afternoon. About 90 minutes later, Moss was at the point but apparently ran out of Amoco on course. His car was disqualified when officials determined that he received a

Lambretta ride and a lift by auto from the pits (rules say drivers must proceed "on foot"). After much pondering, the stewards ruled that the car was out, but the drivers still could compete. Moss entered another car but finished well down the list.

One of the biggest downpours, again at 4:30 that afternoon, increased lap time abruptly but the race plugged on. Shortly before sunset, the clouds cleared, and fans were treated to a brilliant double rainbow over the entire air terminal circuit.

There was at least one spectacular accident in the rain, as a Stanguellini skidded near the auto bridge at the north end of the pits. The car hit several bales of hay, climbed the bridge supports, and landed upside down. Miraculously, driver Bob Rollason was unhurt.

By 8:00, the top ten positions had pretty well been set, and when the cannon boomed at 10:00, it was a Ferrari 250TR that crossed the finish line first. The drivers were listed as Phil Hill, Oliver Gendebien, Dan Gurney, and Chuck Daigh. And despite trouble with the brakes in the final hours, they'd won by a full lap over the second-place car, the team Ferrari of Jean Behra and Cliff Allison. In addition to the Amoco Trophy for their overall win, the Ferrari also netted the Firestone trophy. Again, Behra had torn up the track with the fastest race lap, an average 92.857 mph, eclipsing his mark of the year before. The second-place Ferrari was given $250 and the Earl Nisonger Trophy for being first overall at the six-hour mark of the endurance classic.

Ren Bonnet fulfilled his promise to "defend ourselves honorably for France at the 12 Hours of Sebring . . ." by capturing the index of performance for the third time. The #59 Deutch-Bonnet driven by Parisians Paul Armagnac and Gerald Laurau finished 17th overall. They also were awarded a trophy from Firestone.

As one of his prizes, Hill received a warranty deed to a quarter acre lot in Orange Blossom Lakeshore Estates.

It was a sweeping success both for Ferrari and Porsche with five cars each in the top ten.

Although it was a great race, the conditions took their toll. The average race speed was only 81. 466 mph—the slowest since 1955, and the winners covered fewer than 1,000 miles. The winners made 188 laps for 977.6 miles. However, a new record was set as 48 cars finished the race. Again, the track claimed a life. Edwin P. Lawrence was killed when the Maserati 300S he was driving wrecked at the hairpin during night practice. Accounts say he missed the turn, flipped several times, and died in the flaming wreckage.

Gilbert Johnson, one of the AC Bristol mechanics, died in an off-track mishap south of Sebring the preceding Thursday night. According to reports, the 22-year-old Savannah, Georgia, resident was driving one of the entries when it collided with a pickup truck driven by a Lake Placid woman. Accounts indicate that a passenger, identified as 24-year-old Lonnie Rix, who was to have driven the car in the race, escaped with only a laceration of the chin.

The Sebring fans were learning that sports car racing was an exciting, but dangerous sport. Peter Collins, who had won the event the year before driving a Ferrari with Phil Hill was killed in a subsequent mishap at the German Grand Prix in the summer of '58. He'd held the lead for more than half the race and crashed with just four laps remaining. Collins, known as one of the "Big Three" of Britain, has won both the Buenos Aires and Sebring races, and also had finished first at Silverstone. His death came just one month after the demise of another Sebring stalwart—Luigi Musso.

In January 1959, Englishman Mike Hawthorne was killed while on a "pleasure drive" on a country road. Later that year, the roster of Sebring alumni would be depleted even further, as word came that Jean Behra had been killed in the Berlin Grand Prix (a preliminary for the German G.P. where he was the defending champion). Behra skidded off a wet track and into a flagpole. The force of the impact broke the Porsche in half, and the vehicle burned.

Killed the same day in a French competition was Ivor Bueb. Bueb was a two-time winner of *Le Mans*, and a front-runner in the 1959 12 Hours of Sebring with Stirling Moss. He suffered severe chest and internal injuries when his Cooper hurtled into a ditch during a race for Formula-Two cars in Auvergne.

Following the 1959 '12 Hour' race, attention was turned to the upcoming Formula-One competition dubbed The Grand Prix of the United States. Alec Ulmann revealed at a meeting of the local Lions Club that the CBS Television Network planned to broadcast the event. There would be TV cameras mounted on the Jaguar Tower, atop the WWII parachute loft, and on the back of the course to chronicle the action "for the millions of television viewers." He noted that just as the '12 Hours' kicks off the sports car season, the F1 race would end the grand prix season, and could well decide the driver's championship.

Ulmann made many of his announcements to the Sebring Lions Club. And the accounts subsequently were published in the *Highlands County News*. The group was the first to construct a permanent concession stand at the track—something for which Ulmann complimented them. They responded by making him an honorary Lion, able to represent their division "anywhere in the world."

While plans continued for racing at the track, the Sebring Firemen, Inc. cemented their agreement for the raceway. They convinced the Sebring City Council to extend their lease on the track for eight years, to 1975.

Alec Ulmann from the 1959 program. Reprinted with permission of the Sebring Historical Society.

SEBRING: THE FIRST DECADE

Committee chairman Kenneth Wilson said it would result in the assurance of two worldwide races at the Air Terminal into the mid-seventies and would enable promoters to make long-range plans for the event. At the April meeting, Wilson gave the city fathers a complete update on plans for the Formula-One race, as well as the upcoming Southeast regional drag races to be held there the following month.

Despite their unpleasant experience with rain the year before, the Seven-State Regional Drags were back at the end of May. It was sponsored by the South Florida Timing Association, The Sebring Firemen, and the Highlands County Sherrif's Office, drawing some pretty big names. The most notable was Don Garlits—fans were chattering on whether or not he'd be able to top the record 186.66 mph quarter mile run he had set earlier that year in Brooksville.

There was over $1,000 worth of gold and silver trophies to be given away to the winners. Fans could take a gander at them at Leona's Dress Shop on the circle, where they were on display. The Top Eliminator trophy was sponsored by the Coca-Cola Bottling Company, and there also was a top time award, sponsored by the Crondek Company—a maker of timing equipment. The big prize was an all-expense paid trip to the National Hot Rod Association finals to be held in Detroit, Michigan, on Labor Day. Two trips would be given, one to the Top Eliminator and the other to the Little Eliminator.

Last year's Regionals winner at Sebring, Ed Garlits of Tampa (Don's brother), reached the finals at Oklahoma

City, but fell to the national champion Buddy Samson of Phoenix, Arizona.

But just as in sports car racing, there were also accidents in straight-line competition. 33-year-old William Henry Frazier was killed a week before the regionals in an accident at a dragstrip near Tampa. The Sebring Body Works employee was running the quarter mile there when his brakes apparently locked "causing his converted racing car to flip end over end several times."

He was dead on arrival at Tampa Hospital. Track officials estimated his car may have been going as fast as 140 mph when it went out of control. Ironically, Frazier and another local dragger, Bil Sircy, had a car ready for a run at the Regionals. New reports indicated the men believed their chevy-powered Sircy-Frazier special could turn the course at an average 128mph.

There is no indication on how many fans showed up for the race, but to almost no one's surprise, Don Garlits captured the Top Eliminator category. He did not break his record, but thrilled fans with a final run of 172.41 mph (9.351 seconds). Garlits turned in a 169mph average on his second try but had to shut down the engine halfway through the course when a pinion gear broke. Ollie Olsen of West Palm Beach won the Little Eliminator title, and the Regional Queen selected was a Miami woman—Miss Illona Norman.

As summer wore on, press accounts began to set the scene for the upcoming Formula-One race. It was to be the first time that grand prix cars had run in the United States since 1937.

There were four top drivers who could capture it all at Sebring: Australian Jack Brabham, Tony Brooks of England, former Sebring winner Phil Hill, and the bearded Swede Joakim Bonnier. It was felt when it came down to it, Hill might have the edge, as he was familiar with the Sebring circuit.

In September, the *Highlands County News* began running Don O'Reilly's column "Inside Auto Racing." He intimated that Stirling Moss was the inside favorite to overtake Brabham at Sebring's December race, and indeed, would be bringing a new rear-engined test car that was being fabricated for the 1960 season. In October, O'Reilly pumped the series by revealing that 1959 Indianapolis winner, Roger Ward, would bring a modified American-built midget car for the competition, and that 12 Hour veteran, Lance Reventlow, was working on a new F1 car called the Scarab that he would bring to the inaugural Grand Prix of the United States.

Even though the race weekend would be considerably shorter than the traditional 12 Hours celebration, at the end of October, the Sebring Chamber of Commerce Accomodations Committee was in high gear seeking rooms. This time, they had set rates for specific kinds of rooms, to keep the prices somewhat uniform.

Rooms with a double bed/shared bath $8 twin beds/shared bath $10.

Rooms with a double bed/private bath $10 twin beds/shared bath $12.

As November rolled around, sportswriters began to speculate who would win the drivers' crown and what they would have to do to earn it. Brabham was the odds-on favorite, being the point leader. Stirling Moss could win it if he both won the race and set the fastest race lap. Tony Brooks could win, but it would be a long shot. He would have to win, set the fastest race lap, and both Brabham and Moss would have to perform poorly in the race. Air France offered a trophy for the driver who set the fastest lap during competition.

It was also announced that there would be a couple of supporting races for the three-day event. First, there would be a competition for so-called "Formula Juniors," or F2s. These would be single-seat racers, but not as high powered, with engines limited to 1100cc. The veteran racer and car fabricator, Alfred Momo, was put in charge of this event.

Also, there would be a two-hour race for compact cars. It would be the first such event to be internationally sanctioned. Promoters claimed that the competition "would settle once and for all the question of imports vs domestics." There would be two classes—engines under 2.8 litres with an f.o.b. price of no more than $3,000, and from 2.8 to 4.5 liters with an f.o.b. price of no more than $5,000. The race would be run Saturday morning from 9:30 to 11:30, just prior to the Grand Prix of the United States.

The USGP would comprise 42 laps around the 5.2-mile course, a total of 218.4 miles. There had been some discussion of a 250-mile race, but the experience at Monza, Italy, showed that fuel and wear on the cars might be too much of a problem. Officials did not want oversized gas tanks on the speedsters.

Well over $100,000 was spent by Ulmann on starting and travel expenses for the world-class drivers who would appear. It was a who's who of racing including two-time Sebring winner Phil Hill, Indy 500 winner Roger Ward, and Jim Rathman who was a runner-up at the brickyard, and there was Dan Gurney—the expert's choice for rookie of the year, plus Kansan, Masten Gregory. As noted previously: Sweden's Joakim Bonnier, the American ex-patriate Harry Schell, another Sebring Alumni now living in France, and the German Wolfgang Von Tripps. Englishmen Stirling Moss, Roy Salvadori, and Clifford Allison also planned to race.

Most spectators were there to see the Australian, Jack Brabham. The newcomer's dirt track techniques had excited *aficionados* throughout his first full season. On race day, there were 21 cars and drivers entered for the feature event, representing England, America, France, Germany, Argentina, Australia, and Venezuela. There also were 26 cars for the compact cars' supporting race, the most notable may have been the Falcon entered by Jim Blackman Ford. With that, he became the first local firm ever to enter a car in a Sebring race. He hired the New York sportswriter Denise McCluggage—another Sebring veteran—to drive the car.

The car was actually a showroom model that was pressed into service, when the Ford Motor Company transport was in an accident on its way to Sebring from Detroit. Apparently, company officials sent their mechanics into the Blackman dealership to convert the car for racing. They did a pretty good job—it finished second in its class.

The sedan race had its own line-up of notables, not the least of which was Glen "Fireball" Roberts.

Naturally, the city had its usual round of social events. There were two dances, one was at the Kenilworth, and the second Grand Prix Ball was hosted by the Sebring Junior Women's Club at the municipal pier. Music again was provided by The Sandpipers from Lakeland.

There also was the crowning of another beauty queen. Barbra Klingbiel, an eighteen-year-old German girl working at Cypress Gardens as a skier took the honor. The lovely hazel-eyed brunette had been in the US about a month. She was spotted at the World Water Ski Tournament in Milan, Italy, by Dick Pope Jr. One alumnus who would not be there was Prof. Dean Fales. He was one of the originals from the early days of the Sebring '12 Hour' race. He would have to miss this inaugural Formula 1 event, being confined to his home in Kennebunkport, Maine, with a case of the gout.

News reporters arrived from all over the world to cover the event. The first on the scene was Frank Butler from London's *News of the World*. The man who would have taken the award for coming the farthest—if there was such a trophy—probably would have gone to Robert Perrier. He reportedly wrote for the *Revue Automobile Africane* from Casablanca, Morocco. Others included: Eugen P. B. Morosov and Nina Pavlosky, for *Auto Motor* out of Belgrade, Yugoslvia, and Omar Medici, a reporter for *El Pais* from Montevideo, Uruguay.

The press was furnished with a pair of $15,000 mobile homes by Viking Manufacturing, who also fed the corps with the help of the local Winn-Dixie and Kwik Chek grocery stores.

The USGP drivers were competing for cash as well as glory. First place received $6,000, second $4,000, third $2,000, fourth $1,000, fifth $750, and sixth $500. The winner also would receive a homesite at the Orange Blossom Lakeshore Estates housing development as did '12 Hour' winner, Phil Hill.

During practice, Moss shattered the Sebring course record, turning the 5.2 mile track in three minutes flat, an average speed of 104 mph. Walt Hansgen, noted as ". . . a foremost Jaguar specialist . . ." turned the fast lap in the sedan race at 3:55.2, or 78 mph.

The Cooper Climaxes of Moss, Brabham and Schell were first on the grid, and when the green flag dropped, it was Moss who took the point. By lap ten he had built a 10-second lead. It was short-lived though, the Englishman's transmission failed, dropping his car from the competition.

It was then that Jeff Brabham and teammate Bruce Mclaren headed the pack, running 1-2. But what nobody knew was that Brabham's car had a minor fuel leak that was slowly draining his tank. The car ran out of gas just 400 yards from the finish line.

Mclaren went on to win the race, with Brabham pushing his vehicle the final distance for a 4th place finish, and the world driver's championship. It was half an hour before doctors would allow the totally exhausted Brabham to pose for news photographers.

Motive Power for Sebring. Key men John Goodman, L. W. Moore, Alec Ulmann, Reggie Smith, and Tom Aldridge keep the event turning over at top revs. Goodman, Moore and Aldridge are top management at American Oil Co., sponsors of the race. Reprinted with permission of the Sebring Historical Society.

Motive power for Ulmann. The beautiful DKW 1,000 Sports Coupe is official pace car for Sebring 1959 and will carry Alec Ulmann, Race Director, on his numerous tours of the course. Reggie Smith, Race Secretary, has his hand on the door. Reprinted with permission of the Sebring Historical Society.

1960

As the dawn of a new decade began to break over America's oldest sports car endurance race, the town was in full bore celebration. Even though the first 12-hour race wasn't held until 1952, many references were made to the 1960 race as "10th Anniversary," hearkening back to the 6-hour Sam Collier Memorial held on New Year's Eve of 1950. Much of the infrastructure of the race from walk-over bridges to pit and broadcast facilities had been in place and honorarium ranging from grand marshal to beauty queen were well established.

As always, the pre-race ball was an enormous success. Again, staged by the Junior Women's League of Sebring, it featured a tropical theme with music from the Fabulous Sandpipers, with Jack Tew as the master of ceremonies. The floor show was provided by Ben Eastman who sang, with his wife accompanying him on the marimba. Alec

Ulmann ushered in the new "electronic era" by announcing that the scorekeeping in 1960 would be tabulated by the up-and-coming new technology—a RAMAC 305 computer. Valued in the neighborhood of a million dollars, the computer arrived from Squaw Valley, New York, where it had been used in the Olympics.

"The computer ushers in a new era of strategy in sports car racing," Ulmann told reporters. "For the first time, drivers will know their official standing while the race is still in progress."

As advanced as it was, the human element still was involved. As cars completed a lap, an operator would trigger one of two special Longines quartz clocks, which then would print out the car's time in hundredths of a second. That information then would be placed on an IBM card and transmitted IBM data transceivers along telephone lines to the RAMAC, which was located next to the press section. There, the computer would compile the standings—reports would be issued about every 30 minutes and data subsequently given to pit crews and journalists.

"This computer can store up to five million characters on 50 whirling discs," Ulmann said. "It can retrieve information in less than a second."

The idea was that shortly after the race, a lap-by-lap report would be printed out with vital statistics and each car's performance. It took a crew of 50 IBM techs to assemble the machine, which was kept under armed guard at the Sebring airport. Special electric lines for the set-up were installed by Florida Power crews. Reportedly, it took up an entire pit stall.

The year 1960 also marked the first appearance of the Goodyear blimp at the race. It cruised high above the crowd, flashing messages—including the progress of the race—on its electronic message board, ostensibly aided by data from the new computer system.

In addition to the '12 Hour' classic, two support races would be offered on Friday preceding.

First would be a Formula Junior sprint—which had run the year before, followed by a 4-hour endurance race for smaller GT cars (under 1000cc). Because of increasing press interest in the race, the Viking Manufacturing Company provided mobile homes as press accommodation through their local distributor, Sebring Trailer Sales. In addition to the accommodations, Viking also provided breakfast, lunch, and dinner to the throng of reporters and cameramen. The press also was treated to a Friday night, invitation-only party at Placid Lakes Clubhouse, hosted by August Tobler and the Camordi US Racing Team. Press headquarters again was established at City Pier "because of the beautiful site," and in an effort to help the ever-increasing crush of fans, members of the Sebring Rotary Club manned an information booth at Circle Park.

Early headlines ballyhooed the battle anticipated between manufacturers Ferrari and Maserati. British driving great Stirling Moss was to lead a three-car team of 2.8-litre "bird cage" Maseratis fielded by Camoradi USA. The driver line-up was a veritable who's who of auto racing including Dan Gurney, Caroll Shelby, Masten

Gregory, Roger Ward, and George Constantine. Ferrari, on the other hand, brought their new 3-litre Dino V-6 model.

First to arrive for the race was the Hambro Motors Austin Healy team, with their new Austin Healy 3000.

The Red Cross and Civil Defense crews were employed to give driver physicals and staff a first aid station set up in the infield. They did 200 driver physicals and treated 96 fans for maladies ranging from sunburns and fainting to cuts and bruises. The most serious injury was a fall from the grandstands.

An estimated 37,000 fans were on hand at the Sebring Air Terminal when, under bright and sunny skies, 65

An ambulance parked at the ready. The driver had a unique vantage point for the race. Reprinted with permission of the Sebring Historical Society.

drivers bolted for their cars in the now traditional *Le Mans* start. Jack Nethercutt was first away in the No. 8 Ferrari 250TR but held the point for just three laps before being overtaken by Striling Moss in his Maserati T61.

True to their press, the first half of the race was a duel between the Italian marques. Moss had built up a four-lap lead by the six-hour mark and set a new lap record of just over 97 mph around the 5.2-mile circuit—breaking his 1958 record time. But just as dusk was beginning to fall, Moss brought the white No. 23 Maserati into the pits for the last time with a broken transmission box. Walt Hansgen later retired with an engine problem.

When the checkered flag dropped, it was a Sebring tradition—a winner few had anticipated. Oliver Gendebien and Hans Hermann in a little silver 718 Porsche RS 60 had won the race—taking the Amoco Trophy (it was gold that year in honor of the American Oil Company's 100th anniversary), donning the wreath of kumquats and receiving the obligatory kiss from 1060 Miss Grand Prix, Pat Nelson of Silver Springs.

In fact, the drivers admitted they had slacked off the pace a bit in the waning hours of the race to preserve the car on the very tough racecourse. It was the second straight Sebring win for Gendebien, who had taken the checkers in 1959 with teammate Phil Hill in a Ferrari. Gendebien actually had been a last-minute entry, so sudden that newspaper accounts said "there was considerable surprise when he showed up at the starting line."

What nobody could have anticipated, was that the win by Porsche would set the stage for a winning streak unequaled at the '12 Hours' to this day. The race was marred by several events, including an accident that claimed the lives of a driver and a *Tampa Tribune* photographer. Jimmy Hughes reportedly was having problems with his Lotus Elite and could not make the hairpin curve. As the car came down the escape route it went out of control and flipped, striking 23-year-old George Thompson as he was taking pictures of the race. Both men died in the incident.

The Corvette team, who dutifully replaced several pistons midway through the competition and finished the '12 Hour' grind, lost one of their cars Sunday when it burned. It supposedly backfired while a mechanic was working on it and burst into flame.

The four-hour GT endurance support race was a great success. According to reports 29 cars practiced for the event with 17 starters. The checkered flag fell on a Fiat-Abarth 750 driven by American Paul Richards, covering 17 laps at an average speed of 73.9 mph.

Finishing second was a Targa Florio Sprite driven by Stirling Moss. Accounts say he was supposed to have been aided by John Sprinzel, but Sprinzel reportedly did not show, and Moss drove the whole race. Jim Hall was the victor in the Formula Junior race aboard an Elva DKW, averaging 88 miles per hour over the 30 laps on a shortened 2.2-mile circuit.

The trophies were presented in special ceremonies Sunday at the municipal pier.

Amoco was again the official fuel provider, however, that proved to be a problem for a couple of the major competitors—including Ferrari and Porsche—who had their own fuel deals with the Shell Oil Company. Amoco did not return in 1961.

Nevertheless, the race was deemed a wild success, with Walter Cronkite broadcasting from the '12 Hours.' Airport officials announced that 800 planes had set down during the three days of racing and practicing, with half of them landing on Saturday.

It had been rumored that finances could scuttle another Formula One race at Sebring. Publicist Reggie Smith admitted to reporters: "Yes, we have been approached to move the race to California." Several drivers and even the FIA brought pressure, and Smith revealed that the first race had been a money loser to the tune of $12,000 to $15,000.

Three months later it was official. A September announcement in *Inside Auto Racing* revealed that Ulmann would be the promoter, but that the race and the date would be moved. It was set for November 20, 1960, to move it back from the Christmas holiday season.

To Reign Over Races: MISS 12-HOURS OF SEBRING, Sylvia Belcher, will assume her official throne Thursday night at the race bail scheduled "under the stars" at the Sebring Municipal Pier. Queen Sylvia, a Sebring native, is a secretary in a local law firm. Vital statistics: 34-22-35. Reprinted with permission of the Sebring Historical Society.

1961—A Decade in the Books

The 1961, 12 Hours of Sebring would be the tenth 12-hour race on the historic circuit. Noticeably absent was the name of race creator Alec Ulmann. There was no recognition of it as the tenth annual affair in the pre-race activity or in the general pageantry by the community. There seemed to be no real recognition of the decade's worth of history achieved by the event.

As usual, the first information on the upcoming race came in the first edition of the *Sebring News*. It was announced in a January 3 front page article that the Automobile Club of Florida and the Sebring Firemen, Inc. had reached an agreement to stage the competition at the Sebring Air Terminal. The date was set on March 25, and race officials announced that in eager anticipation of the race requests were already being received for reserved seats and parking. Again, as in the past, the event would be sanctioned by the Federation Internationale l' Automobile, with points going toward the Manufacturer's Championship. Sebring would mark the kickoff, followed by Targa Florio, Nürburgring, *Le mans*, The Tourist Trophy of Great Brittan, and the Grand Prix of Pescara, Italy.

According to the news reports, there would be a pair of support races. One would be a four-hour GT race for cars under 1000cc and the second, another Formula Junior race. This time, the Formula Juniors would run their 20-lap affair on the full 5.2-mile course, and not a shortened course as in the previous year.

In true Sebring fashion, the Cameradi team was heralded as the first entry to register for the 1961 race. Among their drivers would be Stirling Moss and Masten Gregory. They would be behind the wheel of a birdcage Maserati. Officials announced that the team would be in Sebring later this year for testing, but no account of such an activity made it to the local media.

In February, it was revealed that the Sebring press officers would be riding around in style. The Saab Automobile Company of Sweden donated four cars as official vehicles. The 3-cylinder, 4-wheel drive cars were given the once-over, lettered up and put to use. Public Information Director Fred Kingsbury took the opportunity to note that hotel requests were coming in more quickly than usual.

Kingsbury was quick to parrot the Ulmann-inspired method of building race enthusiasm by releasing periodic articles about particulars of the teams and their involvement. There also was the announcement of gate and seating prices for the tenth anniversary race, and that spectators would be able to watch the practice sessions at no additional cost.

A previous restriction to only use Amoco fuel had been lifted for the 1961 competition. As the Amoco sponsorship went away, European teams that had been under contract to use another brand of petrol, now were free to return to the '12 Hour' classic.

Articles ensued about the factory Porsche team entering with half a dozen cars. Oliver Gendebien and Hans Hermann would lead an all-star cast of drivers. Ferrari also would return, represented by a dozen cars—including a new rear engine, Dino 246 SP. It had been described as "ugly, brutish and blindingly fast with almost unbelievable roadholding."

On the home front, it was revealed that there would be eight Corvettes in the race. That would represent the most of the GM brand to appear in the lineup since Sebring's 1957 race. Again, John Fitch would head the effort. The 1960 race had been an ignoble effort for him, when Fitch lost a wheel and flipped the Corvette he'd been driving.

Some sibling rivalry was promised for Sebring as well. Stirling Moss would be accompanied to the track by his 26-year-old sister, Pat. A good driver in her own right, Pat Moss was a two-time winner of the European Women's Rally. She and Stirling would drive Aston Healys in the 4-Hour GT support affair that would run on Friday before the '12 Hours.'

Early in March, a provisional entry list for the '12 Hours' was released with 68 cars. In the end, there would be more than 70 hopefuls but only 65 would be permitted to take the green flag. In all, Ferrari—it was announced—would field 10 cars, Porsche eight, Maserati with seven *Tipos* (aka "birdcage"), and Corvette with six entries—all of them privateers.

Apparently, General Motors had made a quiet agreement with other American manufacturers not to assist racing efforts. That being said, there were a lot of high-performance parts that somehow found their way out of Detroit and onto the track.

There also would be numerous other makes including Abarth, AC Bristol, Alfa Romeo, Elva, Lotus and others. One of those was the "Asardo," powered by an engine out of a Pontiac Tempest. Sadly, the innovative Asardo would not make it to the race, having been withdrawn from competition.

A third support race for the weekend was announced in early March. The four-hour American Kart Race of Endurance was added to the Friday lineup, making for two full days of racing. The kart competition would be by invitation only, with as many as 100 of the small vehicles to run a 2.2-mile section of the Sebring course. Within the entry list there would be five separate divisions.

As race week approached, it appeared that most of the action would be centered at the track. There was significantly less of the community involvement that had been a hallmark of Sebring in the past.

The Highlight of Race Week was to be the Race Ball. "Dancing Under the Stars with Charlie Spivak" represented the first real nationally known entertainment to be featured at the event. Spivak himself was a notable jazz trumpet player, who also had some music credits with a couple of 20th Century Fox motion pictures. Sunny Hartford was billed as the band's vocalist.

They performed at the band shell on the Sebring municipal pier, with a dance floor created in front of the stage. The whole production was overseen by the Sebring Junior Women's Club—who also would reap the benefits. Accounts show they decorated the tables with citrus and "bulbs of many kinds." As part of the festivities, Miss Sylvia Belcher officially would be crowned as "Queen of the Race 1961." A publicity photo (in front of an official Sebring Press Saab GT) revealed Belcher was the secretary for a local legal firm, and her vital statistics were listed as 34-22-35.

Only two other off-track events rose to the level of local press coverage. There was a Grand Prix Golf Tournament at the Sebring Golf Course (Ulmann donated the trophies), and a race party attended by local notables at the Sebring Shores Country Club.

As many as 40,000 fans were expected at the Sebring Air Terminal for the race. Then Highlands County Sheriff Broward Coker made no small effort to take care of the traffic. There were Highlands County Sheriff's deputies, police officers from Sebring, Lakeland, Tallahassee, and Miami, as well as Florida Highway Patrol Troopers. The Highlands County Sheriff's Rescue Unit was brought in as were American Legion Auxiliary members from Miami and Lakeland.

Leading up to the race, the paper was littered with announcements from local businesses offering rooms.

They did such a good job, that an article in the Race Week edition of the Sebring News noted that there were 150 rooms still available for fans seeking lodging.

While there was lots of traffic on the ground, there also were many people coming in by air. The Federal Aviation Administration sent a crew to the Sebring Air Terminal to handle the glut of aircraft flying in for the race. They noted that 150 planes landed on Saturday morning alone.

During the course of racing days, the air traffic controllers handled more than 600 aircraft operations. That included an emergency landing by a PBY Catalina that had been enroute from Miami to Little Rock but suffered engine problems and diverted to Sebring.

In the end, everyone earned high marks. Other than the traditional traffic jam in the minutes before the '12 Hours' started, things went smoothly and there were no traffic incidents of note to report.

Published accounts showed that the 1961 Race Week began Monday morning March 20, when registration opened at Race Headquarters in the Sebring Hotel. Sign-ins continued on through Wednesday, with medical and technical inspections on Tuesday.

Wednesday of Race Week marked the beginning of practice. Sessions were scheduled for the small GT cars in preparation for their 4-Hour race, the Formula Juniors as well as sports and GT cars in the '12 Hour' classic. They took to the track again on Thursday when karts also got a chance at the 2.2-mile short course. Thursday night practice again was held for racers slated for the '12 Hours.'

The week was dominated with highs and lows for everyone involved. One newspaper account related the story of Al Rogers and Jim Bailey. They had left Cleveland, Ohio to drive their Morgan GT to Sebring to race. When they left the Buckeye State the weather was sunny and warm. However, it was in the Carolinas that they ran into snow and icy conditions.

It was then they realized they had not put any antifreeze in the car. The engine froze. The pair ordered a new motor. But while it was being shipped in, they made an appeal to any local owners of Triumph or Morgan cars for some spare parts to help get them back up and running. At the time, they were staying with local resident Don Hansen—who handled medical duties at the track. They gave his number, Evergreen 5-8547 if there was anyone who might be able to help.

Honorary starter of the race would be then Florida Governor Farris Bryant. Earlier in the month he had declared it "International Sports Car Race Week" in the Sunshine State. The official proclamation had glowing words about the Sebring race and the international notoriety it had brought to Florida.

It read:

> WHEREAS, the State of Florida because of its unexcelled year-round climate and excellent highways has attracted national and international attention to sports car activities, and

> WHEREAS, great sportsmanship is demonstrated among the various drivers participating in competition, thereby fostering good relations among the countries of the world, and
>
> WHEREAS, the great State of Florida enjoys world-wide recognition because of the only sports car race of its kind in the North American Continent being held at Sebring each year as the Florida International 12 Hour Endurance Race;
>
> NOW, THEREFORE, I, Farris Bryant, by virtue of the authority vested in me as Governor of the State of Florida, do hereby proclaim March 20-26, 1961, as International Sports Car Race Week in Florida.

Drivers would be competing for $20,000 in prize money and the Alitalia Trophy. The Italian airline had replaced Amoco as the race sponsor. They not only footed the bill for the prize money and the trophy. The airline reportedly transported many of the European competitors to the U.S.

As always there were some interesting stories even before the race had started. A couple of the drivers had experienced problems on the public roads.

For instance, Stirling Moss could not drive himself to the track, in as much as his British driving license had been suspended for dangerous driving. Oliver Gendebien had managed to get a traffic ticket on his way to Sebring, having been cited for speeding.

There's also the tale of a Ferrari that showed up on the grid, numbered and ready to go. The only problem was it wasn't a registered entry. What's more, it wasn't the first time. The suspect driver had pulled a similar stunt the year before. Apparently, he'd parked a Fiat at the end of the grid and made a few laps before being discovered by scorers.

These days, fans arrive several weeks before the race, many already have their traditional spots in mind and bring all the necessaries. In 1961, many spectators had the same idea. Fans were setting up a week before the race. Because there was not a for-purpose track as there is now, officials had to go in after the fact and find the fans to sell them tickets. Apparently, a good number of the folks went into hiding to avoid paying the entry fee.

The tenth anniversary Race Week proved to be an exciting one. In addition to practice runs on Wednesday and Thursday, Friday had a full slate of racing action. It began with a 4-hour enduro for GT cars under 1000cc. Many of the drivers who would be in the next day's '12 Hours,' took a busman's holiday, and raced in that one as well. In all, there were 50 cars on the starting grid.

The race commenced with the traditional *Le Mans* start, as drivers ran across the front stretch and jumped into their cars. It ended as the Fiat-Abarth of Harry Washburn took the checkered flag.

The 20-lap Formula Junior—listed as a 1000km event—was won by Charles Kolb—who took the lead at the green flag and never looked back. He easily took the checkers aboard his rear-engine Gemini.

In the debut of the American Kart Race of Endurance at Sebring, 16-year-old Bobby Allen took the overall win as well as first place in the Class B Open division. The 60-kart field represented five classes of racers.

The tenth running of the 12 Hours of Sebring for the Alitalia Trophy started early. Drivers and others began arriving on the track before dawn, so as not to get caught in the monumental pre-race traffic jam for which Sebring was infamous.

The race officially would begin at 10 a.m. There were reports of mechanics working on cars up to the last minute—at least one was still tinkering with the vehicle even as pit crew members pushed it to the grid. As cars lined up for the start, there was a gaggle of drivers, mechanics, crew chiefs, team principals, officials, reporters, and photographers on the front stretch completing their final arrangements before the opening ceremonies.

There were even some last-minute driver changes. Stirling Moss took over the No. 23 Maserati that had been listed to Masten Gregory. Apparently, Moss preferred the front engine car.

To begin the festivities, Ulmann and Governor Bryant took a "Lap of Honor," around the 5.2-mile circuit in a convertible, accompanied by the four Saab press cars with a motorcycle escort. The Sebring Marching Blue Streaks played a number of tunes, including the Star-Spangled Banner in preparation for the start of the race.

The countdown to Sebring began at the one-minute mark, with Official Starter Jesse Coleman doing the honors. When he hit 10 a.m., he shouted "Go!" The pistol was fired and drivers raced across the front stretch and jumped in their cars. Governor Bryant waved the green flag, and the tenth annual race was under way.

For this '12 Hours,' race cars were positioned along the grid according to engine size. The Corvettes were first away and apparently held the lead to the Mercedes-Benz Bridge. But it was Masten Gregory, who had been deposed from his ride by Stirling Moss, who had the lead on the first lap. Moss, meanwhile, was left in the pits with a dead battery—which cost him six minutes at the start of the race.

On the track, Pedro Rodriguez took the point in a privateer Ferrari but on the 30th lap was overtaken by Richie Ginther driving the rear-engine Ferrari. The team held the lead for two hours, but they finally were overtaken again by the Rodriguez brothers in their North American Racing Team Ferrari.

The NART team held the race lead for five hours. It was then Pedro Rodriguez brought the number 17 in for a pit stop. It turned out to be a grueling 17-minute affair while the pit crew repaired the brakes.

The 1961 '12 Hour' race was a brutal one, with the rough track, high traffic, differential of speeds and the heat of the day taking its toll on cars and drivers alike. Cars were retired with blown engines, broken transmissions, severed steering linkages and bad clutches. Bruce McLaren's Maserati T63 was plagued with an oil leak that dripped onto the exhaust system. That caused some to refer to the number 20 as the "smoke bomb." The car ultimately did not finish.

Graham Hill's Maserati's exhaust broke off at the manifold, turning the cockpit into an oven. That car was retired. Despite Phil Hill's Ferrari having overheating issues and cooking him as he drove, mechanics were able to solve the problem, and he drove the Dino to the Victory Circle. Meanwhile, Hill's teammate, Oliver Gendebien, drove the race under duress. He'd twisted his ankle the day before, practicing the jump into the car for the *Le Mans* start.

In the end, only 43 of the original 65 cars finished the race.

At Sebring, things were famous for disappearing as "souvenirs." The 1961 race was no different. Following the race there was a plea in the local paper. William B. Rearden, who had entered an Aston Martin in the race, was in search of the car's left front wheel.

It appears that the Borrani, wire-spoked wheel came off the car at Turn 17 coming into the pits during the race and, having been left unattended for a time, was scooped up as a trophy by "an overenthusiastic fan." Rearden said the factory wanted to look at the part for structural defects. He indicated there would be "no questions asked" should someone return it to the newspaper offices.

In fact, two of the Aston Martin DB4s lost their left wheels during the '12 Hour' grind.

There's no indication that the part ever surfaced.

EPILOGUE/CONCLUSION

In retrospect, the first ten years of the 12 Hours of Sebring represents an amazing series of events that would result in the world class competition that we see today. Alec Ulmann, a relentless promoter, saw an opportunity at an underutilized facility in a small central Florida town. To his great fortune, he stumbled upon a community that had an organization that had both the will and the wherewithal to make it happen.

Moreover, a newly formed group of racers were presented with a chance to enjoy their hobby alongside some of the greatest drivers on the globe. That being said, some of these gentlemen drivers were themselves barons of industry, stars of film, sports, and even other racing series.

All of this came together at an opportune time. It was during Spring Break. That proved to be a great time for college students to find a place to party, and the down time so racers could spend a long weekend at the track.

Despite some of the early financial losses, Ulmann was able to bring in sponsorship and members of the community were willing to take the hit just to be part of the pageantry and sparkle that was the 12 Hours of Sebring.

It was the influx of stars, the accounts in worldwide newspapers and magazines, radio, and television broadcasts, as well as the feature motion pictures of the race that made the 12 Hours of Sebring into a really big deal.

However, those at the Sebring Airfield had a different view of things. Sebring Airport Manager Alan Altvader wrote an overview of the races from his point of view, and it was a "mixed bag."

"When it was proposed to hold a sports car race on the airport property, those interested in the area and its development as a commercial district had no illusions that the race would have any direct benefits in that direction. There were two reasons why the airport administration favored and recommended its use as a raceway, he wrote.

The people of Sebring had not demonstrated any significant interest in the property as an industrial park. It was too far from town for folks to visit and realize the potential. By offering something that would induce the citizens to look at the property, perhaps they could generate some interest.'

The head of one of the principal tenants on the field (the American Industrial Sales Co.) had talked to those who were promoting the race and he enjoyed their company. The men who wanted to run a "road race" on the airport were all men of wealth, and the airport tenant urged everyone to consider the advantages that a race would bring to the community.

Of course, since none of the local gentry had ever had any experience in this type of activity, none could imagine anything but the most benign effects. And, except for a disappointing financial outcome, the first event did not dampen the expectations. It was a short race-six hours. The crowd of only a couple thousand was composed mostly of local spectators and was easily managed and was very orderly.

The volunteer firemen took charge of all preparations and maintained control during the day. As there were no fences, they set up a patrol of men on horseback and in jeeps to prevent people and animals from straying onto the track.

There were no arrivals before the day of the race and everyone left when it concluded, so the entire event was a one-day affair. It was well-handled and left few "bad tastes." The contestants and their friends filled the hotels and restaurants a couple days before and after the race, so the people of town saw a beneficial effect that encouraged the idea of making the race an annual event.

No construction was necessary by way of pits for the racers or seats for the spectators, and the firemen did such an admirable job of management that the airport had little damage or expense. Even the aftereffects were minimal. Since it was only a six-hour event, there was no camping the night before; no lunches; beer or other accommodations during the day, and toilet facilities—'EVERYONE WAS HAPPY.'

The second race was different, however. As it was set up to be twelve hours long, arrangements would have to be made. The layout of the track was changed; concessions were granted for the sale of food, camera film, souvenirs, beer, and other needs.

Since the course was lengthened, additional flagmen and guards were put into service and it became very apparent that there would be demands for more adequate fire and health protection, and for more toilet facilities. The day started out beautifully but, before the starting gun, a cold front moved in and rain fell in torrents.

The workers on the field were purely miserable as they could not leave their posts to get dry and warm clothes, even though the rain stopped. There were not enough workers to relieve them. And the finances were again a disaster, so the race came close to being the last one.

And, from the day the race became a twelve-hour affair, the airport took a beating on every occasion. It started with the failure of the pavement on a curve. Every passing car broke off another piece so that the race officials changed the route of the course and left holes for the airport to repair.

The race "borrowed" fire extinguishers from all the buildings for standby use in the pits and more than half of them left with the racers. This occurred only one year, and the lesson learned probably was worth the cost.

As the race got wider publicity and drew larger crowds, the burden on the airport increased. There was no way in which it could recoup its losses. The firemen were in charge except for the aviation and utilities operations. They granted concessions to the V.F.W., the Eastern Stars, the Lion Club, and all other organizations which earned hundreds of dollars each year but paid the airport no rent or fees.

The race management charged fees for admission, for parking, for seats, for pit privileges, for advertising, and many other materials and services, but the airport had no way to collect for space, water, electricity, damage to streets and buildings or any other expenses.

The race had become an affair that belonged to the organizations in town, without recourse. The power of the race committee and those connected with the race became so great that they built pits, bridges, and fences. They made any and all arrangements (after the first year or two) without so much as a request for permission or approval.

One aim had been accomplished—the people of Sebring took an interest in the airport (for at least one day a year.)

The day following each race, however, the interest left with the crowd. For the first ten races, the removal of trash left by the spectators was the responsibility and expense of the airport. There was always plenty of volunteer help to stage a parade, a fancy pre-race ball, to flag the corners at the race, to man the concessions, etc., but no volunteers or money to clean up after the race.

As the annual affair gained popularity and became a three-day event, patrons began to come early and to camp out on the property. Then the real trouble began. It was considered the duty of the race administration to provide police protection on the day of the race but, before and after was "open house."

After some of the businesses on the field suffered severe losses by thieves, the firms put on watchmen for the duration. But the airport could not afford enough guards to prevent vandalism. The campers broke into city buildings (such as the water plant, storage buildings, offices, etc.) and took anything of value or scattered maps, papers, and records, and used buildings as bathrooms.

To supply fuel for campfires, doors, siding and other wood parts of buildings were removed. In one case, several visitors moved into a vacant building and built an open fire on the wooden floor.

All of the troubles could not be charged to the visitors. On one occasion, a concessionaire complained to the race committee about his water supply. The fire chief knew everything about correcting his problem, so he opened a fire hydrant and let it run a while. When he spun it closed, he blew out joints in the main in six different places. The airport crew worked around the clock for 48 hours to restore water service to the housing area.

The second reason for recommending the use of the field as a raceway was also accomplished. The company executive who relished being seen hobnobbing with the wealthy sports car racers got his wish. The firemen would have taken a $2,000 loss in each of the first two years except that he made up the shortages. As a result, the racers made him an officer of their club, and the firemen noted him an honorary membership in their volunteer organization.

SO, HE WAS HAPPY.

But the race was not something on the asset side of the airport ledger."

Altvader summed it up well. The airport had not financially benefitted from the race in any great way, but had achieved a number of their objectives. Moreover, the love affair of the community with an event that was bringing them international attention had been kindled, and there was no sign of it ceasing any time soon. And indeed, interest has increased as the years have gone by. The 12 Hours of Sebring has kindled hundreds of thousands of fans, increased interest from the media on a wide variety of platforms and hundreds of thousands of dollars in revenue for the track and the community.

But as we shall see, the race overcame more than a few speed bumps in the ensuing decades.

ACKNOWLEDGEMENTS

I would like to take this opportunity to offer my sincere appreciation to some of the folks and entities that have made this book possible.

First, I would like to thank two of the most knowledgeable 'Sebring 12 Hour' historians, Doug Morton and Ken Breslauer who inspired me to research the development of this event. It has transcended being just a race, and has become an international happening the third week of March each year.

I also would like to thank Bill Foster, who has worked diligently to find a tremendous inventory of photos of the race, some of which he has shared here, to help preserve the rich history of the development of the race.

Additionally, the Sebring Historical Society has opened their archives to me, looking through old copies of the Highlands County News and other publications that chronicle the events and people that were instrumental in the development of the '12 Hours.'

There also are a pair of local sites, Home Sweet Sebring run by Chad DuBose, and Sebring The First 50 Years, whose administrators and members have been very helpful in identifying people, places and things much of which has been been buried in the mists of time.

I also would like to mention Ford Heacock III and the new Auto Racing Club of Florida, which also is dedicated to preserving the legacy of this great event.

There are others who I may have overlooked. For that, I apologize, and pledge to recognize them in the upcoming edition of "Sebring, The First Quarter Century."

www.ingramcontent.com/pod-product-compliance
Lightning Source LLC
Chambersburg PA
CBHW070554160426
43199CB00014B/2500